Forex Trading for Beginners

The QuickStart Guide to Successfully Investing and Make Profits in the Foreign Exchange Market with Simple Strategies.

A Step by Step Trading Plan to Control Your Emotions

By Paul Cohen

© **Copyright 2019 - All rights reserved.**

The content contained within this book may not be reproduced, duplicated or transmitted without direct written permission from the author or the publisher.

Under no circumstances will any blame or legal responsibility be held against the publisher, or author, for any damages, reparation, or monetary loss due to the information contained within this book. Either directly or indirectly.

Legal Notice:

This book is copyright protected. This book is only for personal use. You cannot amend, distribute, sell, use, quote or paraphrase any part, or the content within this book, without the consent of the author or publisher.

Disclaimer Notice:

Please note the information contained within this document is for educational and entertainment purposes only. All effort has been executed to present accurate, up to date, and reliable, complete information. No warranties of any kind are declared or implied. Readers acknowledge that the author is not engaging in the rendering of legal, financial, medical or professional advice. The content within this book has been derived from various sources. Please consult a licensed professional before attempting any techniques outlined in this book.

By reading this document, the reader agrees that under no circumstances is the author responsible for any losses, direct or indirect, which are incurred as a result of the use of information contained within this document, including, but not limited to, — errors, omissions, or inaccuracies.

Table of Contents

INTRODUCTION   6

CHAPTER 1: INTRODUCTION TO THE FOREX MARKET   9

Definition and History of Currency Trading   12

Types of Traders   16

Levels of Trading   20

Advantages of Investing in Forex Trading   23

CHAPTER 2: RISK MANAGEMENT   27

The Reality of Forex Trading   28

Strategies for Risk Management   34

Technical Strategies and Session Routines   34

Self-Discipline   39

CHAPTER 3: TRADING PLATFORMS AND TOOLS   42

Brokers   43

How to Open a Forex Account   49

Self-Empowerment and Useful Trading Tools   54

CHAPTER 4: FINANCIAL LEVERAGE — 61

What Is Financial Leverage? — 62

Advantages of Financial Leverage — 65

Risks of Financial Leverage and How to Manage Them — 67

Managing the Risks of Financial Leverage — 69

CHAPTER 5: BASICS OF TECHNICAL ANALYSIS — 72

The History of Technical Analysis — 75

Fundamental Analysis — 78

Tools for Analysis — 81

Technical Analysis Indicators — 86

Applying Forex Market Analysis — 87

CHAPTER 6: STRATEGIES FOR BEGINNERS — 89

Buy Low and Sell High — 94

Stop Loss — 96

Take Profit — 98

Best Currencies to Follow — 100

Compare Currencies — 103

CHAPTER 7: MANAGE YOUR EMOTIONS WITH TRADING PSYCHOLOGY — 105

The Basics of Trading Psychology — 107

Winning and Losing Mindsets in Trading	110
Day Trading or Long-Term Trading?	113
Keep a Daily Diary	116
CHAPTER 8: FOREX SPECIFICS	**119**
Risk-Reward Ratio	120
Types of Orders	121
How Many Pips are Enough?	124
CHAPTER 9: PLAN YOUR DAY	**126**
Get Rid of the Fluff	126
Cut Out Negative People	132
Set Yourself a Goal	133
Get More Sleep	137
CHAPTER 10: TIPS FOR SUCCESS	**140**
Succeeding on Buy and Sell	144
Mistakes to Avoid in Forex Trading	146
CONCLUSION	**153**

Introduction

Congratulations on purchasing *Forex Trading for Beginners* and thank you for doing so. The following chapters will discuss the basics of forex trading and how a new investor can start trading in the forex market. This book will provide you with detailed insight into how the foreign exchange market works and why it is a great opportunity for investors looking to generate significant returns on their investment and diversify their investment portfolios.

Learning how to make your money work for you is a key skill in achieving financial stability and ensuring your financial future. We cannot always count on our ability to work in order to generate money for our needs and wants, time, health and many other circumstances can hinder your ability to make money so having skills on how to use the money you already have to make money will provide you with a much needed safety net in case of any eventualities.

The forex market is an ideal investment avenue. Daily transactions are typically in excess of a trillion US dollars, making it a large market for investors that is also easily accessible and flexible. With a wide range of market analysis tools and resources available for the forex trader to use in developing and enhancing their skills in forex trading, it provides a profitable and sustainable avenue of making money for traders who are disciplined, committed and willing to learn.

This book seeks to equip you with the tools and knowledge necessary to trade successfully in the forex market. Strategies provided on market analysis and risk management are intended to guide you in coming up with a viable trading plan that will ensure that you get the most out of your trading capital in terms of profits.

Success in any sphere of life is enhanced by multi-disciplinary knowledge that builds our understanding of how things work. This is the best way to identify and make use of opportunities to better ourselves and improve the quality of our lives. Forex trading is a great opportunity that you should take full advantage of, whether you are a first-time investor or a seasoned investor looking to diversify your portfolio.

There are plenty of books on this subject on the market, thanks again for choosing this one! Every effort was made to ensure it is full of as much useful information as possible, please enjoy!

Chapter 1: Introduction to the Forex Market

Whether your goal is financial independence or the acquisition of wealth, knowing how to make your money work for you is an invaluable skill for any investor. We work hard to make money for our needs and wants, but even more important than earning money is being able to hold onto it and better still multiplying what we already have.

Regardless of how much money you have in your account if your spending outpaces your income you are not financially independent. Financial freedom entails creating automatic income to sustain you without needing to work, and having more money coming in that you are spending.

Even if you work 60 plus hours a week and make good money, at some point your ability to work might be hindered by age, health or any other unavoidable circumstances. This means that if you solely depend on your ability to work then you cannot guarantee your financial security in the future.

How many pensioners do you know who live on a fixed income after years and years of hard work in their respective careers? Hard work may give you an income in the present but unless you find a way to hold on to your earnings and find ways to make your money work for you, you are bound to face an uncertain financial future. This is where investing comes in.

In order to grow your money, you need to invest it. An investment is a monetary asset that is acquired for the purpose of generating income in the form of profit. Investing requires an outlay of money, time or effort in the present to achieve gains in the future. Investing is a two-faced coin, with one face having returns and the other having risk. All types of investment carry a certain amount of risk as well as the potential for return on investment.

When it comes to investing, time is your best friend. Interest in capital accrues over time so the longer the time you have invested your money, the more interest and returns you can get on your investment. While many people put off investing in an uncertain time in the future or for when they have 'enough money', the truth is that you are never too young or too broke to start investing. The golden rule of thumb when it comes to making your money work for you should be, start where you are with what you have.

The beauty of investing is that there are multiple avenues of investing open to anyone looking to put their money into ventures that will earn returns in the future. From real estate, bonds, mutual funds, options, and forex trading there is no limit to the options available to a willing investor.

Forex trading is increasingly becoming a preferred choice for investments for both new and experienced investors and has gained popularity worldwide. Currency trading is a global market that is worldwide, continuous and characterized by large trading volumes.

Definition and History of Currency Trading

Forex trading refers to the buying and selling of currencies. In essence, the foreign exchange market is a platform for different types of traders in the form of individual investors or institutions such as banks can buy and sell different world currencies. A forex trade transaction is characterized by selling one currency and purchasing another, for instance, you can use US dollars to buy a certain number of Euros depending on the current trading value in the market. The two currencies that characterize the forex trade are referred to as a currency pair.

Currency trading is carried out over an online platform that is referred to as the Interbank market. This market is open 24 hours each day, from Monday to Friday throughout the year. Global daily turnover in the foreign exchange currency market is in excess of US$5 trillion, making the currency trading market one of the biggest markets in the world in terms of value. A typical forex foreign transaction involves a situation where a buyer purchases a quantity of one currency, for example, Euros by another currency such as the US dollar. For instance, you can use US dollars to purchase Euros, similarly, you can purchase US dollars using Swiss Francs. In these trades, the exchange rate will be determined by the values of the buying currency in comparison to the currency being purchased.

For international trade to take place effectively, it is important for countries to have access to a market that enables them to convert local currencies to other currencies, this means that forex trading is an important factor in facilitating trade between different countries. For example, if a company in the United States was to import goods from Germany or any other European country, it can easily pay for the transaction in Euros rather than dollars by converting US dollars into euros.

In forex trade the basic terms used in trading include;

Currency pair: this pair refers to the two currencies that are being traded in a foreign exchange transaction. For instance, if you are trading US dollars for British Pounds then the currency pair, in this case, is USD /BP.

Base Currency: If we take the above currency pair as an example, the base currency is the US dollar which is your home currency or the currency you wish to exchange or sell. This buying currency is also referred to as the accounting currency or the domestic currency.

Quote Currency: In a currency pair the second currency which is being purchased in the trade is referred to as the quote currency. It is usually the foreign currency in the transaction, for instance in our USD / BP currency pair example, the British pound would be the quote currency. In forex trading transactions, the quote currency can also be termed as the counter or secondary currency.

Cross currency pair: In forex trading, not all trades involve the use of US dollars. It is possible for currencies to be traded in the forex market without converting either the base or quote currency into us dollars first. This time of currency pair is referred to as the cross-currency pair.

Pip: In a typical currency exchange there is a difference in the exchange rate between two currencies. The smallest price change that can occur in this exchange rate is referred to as a pip. In most cases, currencies will be priced to four decimal places, meaning that the smallest change will be that of the fourth decimal point.

History of Forex Trading

Currency exchange has always been an important part of trade throughout history. It enabled people from different regions to trade in items such as food, cloth, tools, and many other essentials. For instance, if Egyptian merchants were trading with Turkish merchants, and the Turkish merchant's currency was worth more than the Egyptian currency in terms of value, then the Turkish trader would be able to purchase more goods with fewer coins because the value of his coins would make them superior in terms of purchasing power.

Throughout history, the value of currencies has been set against commonly recognized measures such as gold or silver. Gold was typically used to fix the value of a currency by providing a measure that could equate a certain quantity of gold to a certain amount of money. Silver was also used as a measure of value for different currencies.

As early as the fifteenth century, banks had been opened to facilitate trade between different countries. The year 1880 is considered the beginning of foreign exchange and it saw the established of the gold standard. The gold standard meant that the standard economic unit of account was established based on a fixed quantity of gold. This standard was widely used in the 19th century and as well as in the early part of the 20th century. The Bretton Woods Accord was signed in 1944, to allow currencies to fluctuate within a specific range. A free-floating currency system came into effect in 1971 after the ending of the Woods accord. The volume of trading in the forex market increased significantly from 1970-1973 with the volume of trades being made tripling within those three years. The increase in volume called for a better trading system and this is what prompted Reuters to introduce computer monitors into the forex trading market from 1973. Hitherto the introduction of computers, telephones, and telexes were the main platforms that were used for trading quotes.

By the end of the first quarter of 2010, at least 36% of the trading volume in the forex trading market was attributed to the UK making it the largest foreign exchange trading center at the time. The United States, over the same period, accounted for at least 17% of the global foreign exchange trade while Japan was third in terms of volume with a contribution of 6% of the total traded volume.

Recent years have seen a remarkable increase in the total turnover of forex trade. By April 2010 the turnover of the options and futures market had reached the $166 billion mark. As it stands, over 2% of OTC turnover in foreign exchange is accounted for by forex currency derivatives.

Types of Traders

As one of the biggest financial markets globally, the forex trading market is comprised of different categories of forex traders who buy and sell currencies. These different types of traders use different trading techniques and utilize a variety of software and platforms to facilitate their trading activities. Different forex traders work with different trading strategies while predicting or making speculations in the forex market.

The various trading techniques adopted by forex traders are based on their knowledge of the forex market and the trading strategy that fits their individual objectives. When it comes to foreign exchange trading one of the most important factors that influences and guides trading is time.

On the basis of time, forex traders and trading strategies can be divided into different classes. These include;

1. Day Traders
2. Position Traders
3. Swing Traders
4. Scalpers

Day Traders

A forex day trader is the class of forex traders who ensure that all their trades are concluded and closed by close of business hours. In day trading no positions are left open beyond each particular trading day. This type of trading is established on the ground of entering and exiting a trade position at a very fast rate. This means that volume and liquidity are important factors in day trading. In most cases, financial securities with a small daily range or volume will an ideal market for a day trader. Forex day traders focus on events that cause short-term forex market moves. This makes trading the news a very popular technique in day trading.

Day traders will typically trade based on the information that they acquire from scheduled economic news releases. This includes news such as the economic statistics of a country, corporate earnings, and interest rates. These economic expectations cause significant moves in the forex market when they are met or exceeded and these moves, in turn, generate profits for day traders. The price volatility of a particular currency and its average daily range is an important element in day trading.

Position Traders

Position traders usually trade securities in the forex market by holding a trade position for an extended period of time. This period ranges anywhere from a couple of weeks to months or years. Position traders are not active traders. They initiate few trade positions in an entire year and are therefore less concerned with short-term price fluctuations and the economic news release of the day.

Position traders typically make use of weekly and monthly price action analysis charts to determine how particular security fluctuates. They make profits and returns from the price changes in the primary trends. Position trading is characterized by trades that are performed with emphasis on both fundamental and technical analysis. These trading indicators give position traders a better evaluation of the forex market, and the ability to make better trade decisions.

Swing Traders

Swing traders make profits and returns in the forex market by holding a trade position either overnight or for a period ranging from days to several weeks. Swing traders make use of fundamental analysis, the basic value of a security, price trends, patterns, and technical analysis to identify financial instruments with short-term price momentum. Swing traders trade by the identification of securities which have the most likely possibility to move in a short time frame.

The aim in swing trading is to trade on large price moves on a daily basis by spending a long time monitoring the security in question. The monitoring period can range from weeks to months.

Swing trading usually doesn't involve watching the market in real-time. Swing traders buy securities when the market moves in an upside swing and sell securities when the swing halts, stops or plateaus. They focus on a particular asset and understand the movement that takes place within the asset.

Traders make higher returns and profits in swing trading than in a buy and hold trading. This makes swing trading the best option for those who trade for a living. The level of risk in swing trading is lower when compared to other types of trading.

Scalpers

Scalpers in forex trading are the traders who enter a trading position for a very short time frame with the aim being to make profits out of the shorthold. Scalpers buy and sell securities several times in a day with the intention of making a small percentage of consistent profits out of the market.

The strategy used by scalpers yields more profits when there is high volatility in the market and sufficient market moves. However, there is a certain percentage of risk associated with this trading strategy because a scalper may enter into a trade position from which it is difficult to exit and, in the process, they can be left with an open trade position which may result in loss of profits.

Levels of Trading

Horizontal Levels are a forex trader's basic tool for guiding their trading and enabling them to come up with winning strategies for their trades. Horizontal levels form part of the core principles that most traders use as part of their trading strategies. They provide a trader with an invaluable tool when analyzing charts.

With the help of horizontal levels, a trader can determine vital sections or points on a chart where the market trend is likely to change. This information becomes the guide that the forex trader will use in determining the best entry point into a trade, where a stop limit would be ideal, and when to exit a trade. This information is important because it can make the difference between a winning trade or a losing trade. Successful trades can be executed by drawing the levels of the price changes observed on the charts. Trends can be determined using horizontal levels and once you have a clear indication of the market trends you are then able to make informed decisions in regard to your entry, exit and stop-loss points in a trade.

In most cases, the timing of your entry into a trade will be one of the factors that determine whether you make a profit or loss on your position. When you analyze the points on the chart where the trend changes (swing points) you can be able to predict the direction the trend is likely to take and where the next swing point will be.

For instance, the diagram below shows the position of the swing points in this particular chart.

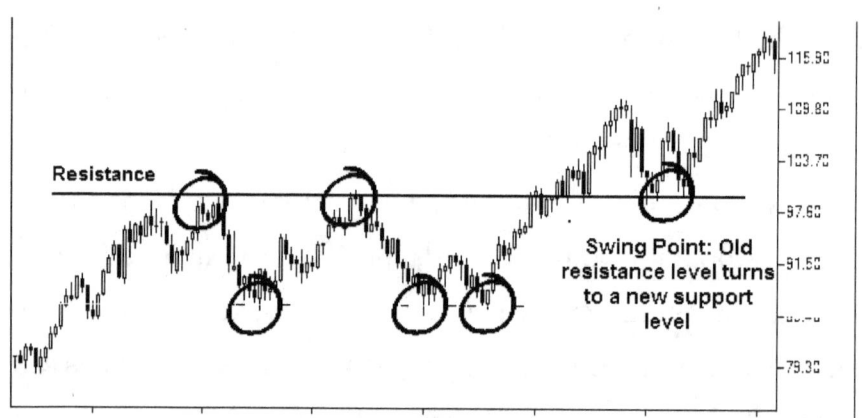

Horizontal levels are a very useful indicator in markets where the price ranges between easily identifiable upper and lower limits as in the chart above. These types of markets are referred to as range-bound markets. When working with range-bound markets, observing the price as it tends towards the lower limit or upper limit can give you an indication of how the price is likely to move.

Advantages of Investing in Forex Trading

Leverage

Investing in foreign exchange creates an opportunity to obtain leverage. Leverage in forex trading can be described as the ability to borrow and trade with more money than your trading capital. Trading capital simply refers to your initial investment or the money you put in your trading account to use for your transactions. In a scenario where you have invested $5 and then borrow leverage at 5:50, then despite the fact that your initial investment was $5, you will have the same returns as if your total investment had been $50. In essence, the goal of leverage is to avail more funds to you to trade with than you would have to work with only your own investment. Access to high amounts of leverage is one of the pulls of the forex market to investors by allowing people to magnify the potential returns on their investment. In markets such as the stock market, no leverage is used.

Flexibility

The beauty of the forex market is that it is always open. When the markets are closing at the end of the day in New York, they are just opening at some other part of the globe. This allows trading to continue 24 hours a day which means that the trader can operate on the schedule that best suits him because he is not tied to local business hours as would be the case in domestic markets. This flexibility in time also means that traders can react to market changes in real-time.

The Foreign Exchange Market Is Easily Accessible

Anyone around the globe can access the forex trade market. Forex markets are available for traders from any part of the globe they only need to observe the local regulations in their country. Access to the market is readily facilitated by forex brokers and financial institutions such as banks. The listing of options and futures on exchanges means that investors can trade in these markets through their futures and securities accounts.

Portfolio Diversification

Investing in foreign exchange provides portfolio diversification benefits to investors. The foreign exchange markets are not related to asset markets so they can provide an alternative for making significant profits and returns on capital when the stock markets are stalled.

There's High Liquidity in Foreign Exchange Markets

When an asset can be converted quickly into cash, that asset can be said to have high liquidity. Foreign exchange trading is one of the markets where substantial sums can be transacted into and out of the market with little change in prices.

Low Costs of Transactions

In forex trading, the cost of a transaction is usually factored into the price. This cost is referred to as the spread. The spread in a forex transaction refers to the margin between the purchase price and the sale price.

There's Profit the from the Rise and Fall of Prices

In forex trading, there are no restrictions when it comes to trading in the direction you expect a market to move in. This type of strategy is referred to as directional trading. In directional trading, when you expect a particular security to increase in value, you can choose to buy the security or take a long position. On the other hand, if you expect a decrease in value, you can sell the security or go short.

Chapter 2: Risk Management

The immense potential to make huge profits afforded to investors by the forex market comes with the risk of losses as well. Investment in any venture is a double-edged sword, it carries the potential for returns on capital, but it also has potential for losses. For any discerning investor, the focus is on retaining your trading capital and then making profits on this amount, if you lose your trading capital then you are essentially out of business.

Safeguarding your money by taking steps to ensure that your investment yields profits should be an investor's primary goal. When you venture into investment the aim is primarily to make your money generate more money for you in the form of profits. Yet many investors lose money hand over fist by failing to take the time to understand the markets they are getting into and how best to trade in them.

While no investment can be 100% risk-free, taking steps to safeguard your investment and trading wisely can greatly minimize the possibility of making losses in your investment.

The Reality of Forex Trading

Your profit opportunities as an investor in the forex trade will come hand in hand with the potential for losses. Forex trading is a profitable venture for the discerning trader but is also subject to risks that are occasioned by factors such as market fluctuations. Changes in market trends can cause differences in the currency exchange rate between your entry point into a trade and your exit point. These kinds of fluctuations inevitably impact the price the security which in turn determines whether your trade will be profitable or a loss.

A central market is not required in forex trading meaning that execution price is determined by the forex dealer. The investor, in this case, has to work with the price set by the dealer. In effect when a trader gets a fair price from the dealer he increases his margin of potential returns but on the other hand. If the price is not favorable his potential margins are diminished.

Most traders tend to depend on online platforms for their trading activities. Since electronic and online internet-based systems are susceptible to breakdowns and dysfunction periodically, trades can be affected during the downtimes. System failure can hinder you for a certain period of time from either entering new trades, executing existing orders, or modifying or canceling the existing trades.

In forex trading just like in other types of investments, investors should be vigilant especially beginners who are not familiar with this market. It is important to guard your investment against fraud. The increase in the interest in forex trading has inevitably led to a significant increase in foreign currency scams, and therefore due diligence is required before engaging in forex trading.

Risk Management

Assessing the market should be the primary consideration for both new and seasoned traders. Successful trading will only happen if you can effectively safeguard your trading capital or initial investment. Losing your trading capital means that you will not have money to trade with. For this reason, any trader intending to be successful in foreign exchange trading has to make risk management a priority because, in the long run, your ability to manage risks will mean the difference between success and failure.

When it comes to managing risks in foreign exchange trading, the main principles that every trader should adhere to are;

- Understanding the main risks involved in forex trading
- Studying those risks
- Identifying strategies to minimize the risks
- Using these strategies consistently.

Ultimately, forex trading is a numbers game and this means that to get maximum returns on your investment you have to find a way to tilt every little factor to your advantage. Trading without risk management is akin to gambling where you will be leaving your fate to luck and chance. While gambling may net you some money here and there, more often than not you are likely to end up in losses.

Risk management works by controlling your losses and increasing your profitability. But before you can look at risk management, you must first understand the main risks that are associated with forex trading. These risks include;

Rapid Market Fluctuations

Many factors can alter market direction and influence trends in the currency exchange market. Economic releases, policy changes and political declarations in major markets can all affect trends and currency prices. Market fluctuations can, therefore occur within seconds. For instance, a major central bank announcing significant changes in interest rates can result in huge gaps in the trade chart within seconds. Similarly, economic stability and political pronouncements can influence currency values and affect trades.

These kinds of pronouncements and decisions are not possible to predict so the only way to mitigate their effects would be to set up automated stop mechanisms such as stop-loss that can be used to close trading orders. Though stop mechanisms may not help you avoid losses entirely, they can reduce the level of losses significantly.

Leverage Effect

Access to leverage is one of the main reasons that investors choose to invest in forex trading. Leverage provides an investor with the opportunity to borrow and trade with more money than their starting investment. Leverage, therefore, creates a situation where a trader can make more money than his initial investment would have allowed him to. However, this also means that you stand to lose more if the market goes against you.

In principle, the higher the leverage, the faster the rate at which you can gain profit or loss. When your level of borrowing is too high which occurs when you choose a leverage level with a risk too high for you to manage this means that you have over leveraged yourself. Trading with smaller investments helps you avoid over-leveraging though it will also reduce your potential profit. It is therefore important to use a leverage level that is proportional to your trading account volume and that presents a manageable risk.

Wrong Assessment of the Market

Market fluctuations are common in forex trading. This creates a situation where orders typically start in the negative because the cost difference between the bidding and asking price is deducted on opening a trading order.

Naturally, market assessments will not always be correct because you cannot always predict market changes and fluctuations. Your market assessment cannot always be right and these means that you should expect to lose profit once in a while. You can, however, control how much you stand to lose by putting in place a stop-loss limit at the final point at which a loss would be acceptable.

Market Gaps

Market gaps occur when there are significant leaps in price. When markets are closed leaps in price can occur creating gaps. Even when markets are open and unexpected news or policy releases cause drastic price changes, there can be huge gaps between the expected and actual closing points in the market.

These market gaps are risky because they reduce the effectiveness of automated limits like the stop loss which are intended to control loses. In a situation where there is a market gap, the stop loss mechanism can only close trades at the next quote that is available after the price jump.

Ultimately, market gaps can be positive or negative, in case of positive spillage you will get more profit than your projection, while on the other hand, negative spillage will cause you more loses than would have been incurred in normal circumstances.

Strategies for Risk Management
Technical Strategies and Session Routines

1. Only Invest Money You Do Not Need

The first rule to consider in currency trading, or any other kind of investment, is to not risk money that you cannot afford to lose. This is because there is no guarantee in forex trading and therefore your trading capital can be multiplied when you make a profit or loss when the markets go against you.

It is easy to assume that it will not happen to you but even while taking appropriate measures to ensure success, risking money that you need to live is financial irresponsibility. This is especially important to remember for beginners who may be willing to risk everything to make a quick buck.

When you trade with funds that you cannot afford to lose, you will inevitably put undue pressure on yourself. The net result of this is that the emotional stress will impact your trading leading you to overtrade or overleverage yourself which will be increasing the probability of losing your investment and ending up with losses.

The foreign exchange market is prone to fluctuations which can make it volatile and unpredictable. Trading reasonable amounts from your disposable income is a wise strategy especially for beginners who are just getting to know how the forex market works.

2. Stop-Loss - Knowing Your Limit

An accurately positioned stop loss can react to market changes quicker than a trader would intervene. This makes Stop loss an invaluable risk management tool for forex traders. Rapid market movements mean that prices can change in an unpredictable manner within short periods of time. This is a common occurrence in volatile markets and in such cases, the stop loss becomes an ideal mechanism for limiting your exposure in terms of possible losses. In these cases, a stop loss can be used to close a trade at the indicated final level at which you can accept a loss, this will in effect minimize your risk exposure due to volatile market changes.

Choosing an effective and appropriate stop-loss limit requires you to consider the following factors;

- The length of the trade, longer trades are generally riskier.

- The expected price and duration you will need to reach it.

- The size of your account and current balance.

- The number of open positions you have.

- The size of your order and whether it matches your, account balance and time frame.

- The general market sentiment at the time of entering the trade (for instance, is it volatile, awaiting news or other external factors?)

- The time frame available before the market closes. (for instance, is it almost weekend?)

3. Limit Your Risk per Trade

Risk management involves considering your trading capital when making trades. To minimize your risk exposure, you should only invest a limited percentage of your trading capital in each given trade: For instance, it is generally recommended that you commit 2% or less of your available capital per trade. For example, if your trading capital is $5,000 then you can risk set your maximum allowable risk per trade at $100.

4. Choose Your Leverage Wisely

Leverage allows investors to trade more money than your initial deposit. The Forex market is a highly liquid market and this makes it possible for leverage to be applied in forex trades. When using leverage, your potential profits are significantly increased by the availability of more money which you can use to trade more, but in the same way, the same multiplication factor applies to your potential losses. The more leverage you have the greater the risk is. It is therefore important to understand how leverage works and its impact on your overall performance and trading.

It is tempting to over-leverage yourself in order to make significant profits, but over-leveraging means that even one quick change can wipe you out.

5. Take Currency Correlations into Account When Making Your Trade

To develop winning strategies and enhance your chances of success in the forex market, you should have a clear grasp of your exposure by knowing the correlation between currency pairs (the two currencies to be exchanged). In forex, currencies are traded in pairs and it is necessary to know how they relate to each other. You will find that there are currency pairs that move in sync in the same direction while others will tend to evolve in different directions.

Correlation of currency represents the measure of the relationship in terms of movement between one currency and the other. When two currencies are positively correlated, they generally move in a similar direction, while currencies that are negatively correlated to each other move in opposite directions.

For example, trading EUR/USD, the AUD/USD, and the GBP/USD currency pairs which have the same counter currency means that they will generally evolve in the same direction because they are positively correlated. In this case, your portfolio will tend to strengthen when the USD is strong and weaken proportionately when it weakens.

6. Keep Your Risk Consistent

It is tempting to risk more per trade when you start making profits. This magnifies your risk exposure. It is important to keep your risk consistent and avoid becoming overconfident. Becoming overconfident and less risk-averse can cause you to change your trading plan and disregard risk management techniques. Sticking to your trading plan ensures that you are consistently managing your risks and are in full control of your investment plan.

7. Set Your Ratio of Risk/Reward at a Minimum of 1:3

A risk-reward ratio measures the distance between your entry point in the trade and your limit orders which are the stop loss and take profit orders. Setting a risk/reward ratio improves your chances of success in the long run by enabling you to set limit orders that protect your trading capital.

If you are using a risk-reward ratio (RRR) of 1:3 it means that you are risking 100 pips to win 300 pips. In this case, the margin between your point of entry and your stop-loss is 100 pips. The margin between your take profit and your entry point is 300 pips. The risk-reward ratio is used in determining and comparing the difference between your point of entry and the stop-loss and take-profit orders.

Self-Discipline

Forex trading like any other investment requires commitment and planning to achieve success. If you are going to commit your money, it follows that you should train yourself to do the necessary to ensure the profitability of your investment. Self-discipline in forex trading is achieved by:

- Creating a winning trading strategy

- Changing the trading plan as needed

- Executing and following the strategy effectively.

A trading strategy forms the foundation of a trader's success. A trading strategy creates guidelines for the investor to follow when making and executing trades as well as when stopping orders. It serves to provide a basic road map that details how the trader will engage in the forex trade market. Key things to consider when coming up with a trading strategy include determining;

- The minimum length of time per trade
- The maximum length of time per trade
- The frequency of trades to be made
- Trading hours
- The list of trading instruments you will need

Listing a set of rules and procedures to follow will develop your trading and enable you to practice discipline.

Part of self-discipline in trading means avoiding overconfidence and loss aversion as well as avoiding over risking on a particular trade. Using measures such as stop-loss enables you to trade based on a predetermined strategy and emotional influences out of the equation. This is what enables you to stick to your trading plan.

To exercise discipline in forex trading, Patience is a crucial element that you need to develop. Market fluctuations in the currency exchange market are a normal occurrence and should not cause you to change your trading plan. When it comes to trading successfully in forex, take your time and understand the

- No Dealing Desk Broker

- Market Makers

- Electronic Communications Network Brokers (ECN)

No dealing Desk Forex Broker (NDD)

The NDD forex broker does not have a dealing desk. This type of broker usually provides the best quotes. They get these quotes from a variety of forex quote providers.

Multiple quote providers usually present their best markets to the No Dealing Desk broker. The broker then executes the trades and fills orders for the clients. The No Dealing Desk broker usually charges a commission on the trades made or increase the bid/offer spread in order to make some profit on each trade.

tools that will improve your chances of success and make the winning trades possible.

Ultimately, long-term trades will require a higher level of self-discipline to stick to the trading plan. Success in forex trading stems from knowing the best time to trade and when to stay away from the market. When you are working with a small trading account bigger risks and frequent trading will help to maximize returns or profits. However, bigger trading accounts call for smaller risks and less trading.

Chapter 3: Trading Platforms and Tools

Forex trading provides an opportunity for people to invest in the currency exchange market. Identifying the right trading platform and tools will be instrumental in the success of your investment. A learning trader just starting out in forex trading requires a user-friendly interface, a stable environment that offers flexibility and availability of tools that they can use for trading. When it comes to trading planning, patience and will be your greatest allies.

Trading profitably in the forex market can be difficult b you develop a trading plan, get well acquainted with forex trading tools, and continuously increase your kno of the forex trade, you will have made significant steps to becoming a successful trader and realizing great retur your investment.

Brokers

Forex brokers are the pathway through which investors access to the forex market Brokers offer investors conven terms and a good broker will be a great asset for you in y trading journey. Choosing the right broker will mean difference between succeeding or failing in your forex trad venture. When choosing a broker, you should consider it yo first and most important trade in the forex market. An invest entrusts their trading capital to the broker, with the intent trading with that capital and then being able to withdraw i when they want to take their returns.

Different brokers will generally have their own unique way of dealing with transactions and executing orders. When determining which type of forex broker to use on the basis of their forex quotations, there are three main categories of brokers;

Market Makers

A market marker broker-dealer firm holds a number of positions on its books for a particular pair of currencies in order to facilitate trading in that currency pair. In this way, they take on some risks themselves. A forex market maker category of broker will provide its clients with a two-sided market that will be created by a specialist forex trader who operates in the broker's own dealing desk. The broker in effect takes up the other side of any given trade. They can achieve this by selling on their offer price or buying on their bid side

This type of broker generally purposes to obtain part of the spread and trade enough volumes on either side of the market. When the market marker is executing big trades, they can choose to offset the trade immediately if they predict a market move against the trade.

Electronic Communications Network Brokers

In this category of brokers, electronic communications networks are used to give clients direct access to other traders in the currency markets. An Electronic Communications Network broker avails an electronic trading interface that can be used by traders and other forex market participants to execute trades. In this case bids and offers are made through the electronic platform provided by the ECN broker.

Since this category of brokers are able to obtain price quotations from different market participants they can offer their clients tighter bid/ask spreads than would be possible in ordinary circumstances. ECNs brokers can also give some degree of anonymity to the trader which is an advantage for traders who do not wish to disclose that they are on the bid.

Electronic Communications Network brokers' spreads are usually slim when compared to those used by everyday brokers. They charge a commission on each trade executed.

Now that you have an understanding of the distinction between the types of brokers available, the next step is to identify which broker will suit your personal needs and trading goals. To do this, need to consider the following factors;

- **Consider your needs**

Before looking at brokers it is important to assess your own trading needs. What will your frequency of trading be? Are you looking to trade small moves, or capture bigger moves?

If your focus is on day trading and to capture small moves, consider an ECN broker. With an ECN broker, the spreads are narrow which will be significant when entering small trades. Similarly, if your preferred mode of trading is scalp trading, an ECN broker will be ideal.

tools that will improve your chances of success and make the winning trades possible.

Ultimately, long-term trades will require a higher level of self-discipline to stick to the trading plan. Success in forex trading stems from knowing the best time to trade and when to stay away from the market. When you are working with a small trading account bigger risks and frequent trading will help to maximize returns or profits. However, bigger trading accounts call for smaller risks and less trading.

Chapter 3: Trading Platforms and Tools

Forex trading provides an opportunity for people to invest in the currency exchange market. Identifying the right trading platform and tools will be instrumental in the success of your investment. A learning trader just starting out in forex trading requires a user-friendly interface, a stable environment that offers flexibility and availability of tools that they can use for trading. When it comes to trading planning, patience and will be your greatest allies.

Trading profitably in the forex market can be difficult but once you develop a trading plan, get well acquainted with the key forex trading tools, and continuously increase your knowledge of the forex trade, you will have made significant steps towards becoming a successful trader and realizing great returns on your investment.

Brokers

Forex brokers are the pathway through which investors gain access to the forex market Brokers offer investors convenient terms and a good broker will be a great asset for you in your trading journey. Choosing the right broker will mean the difference between succeeding or failing in your forex trading venture. When choosing a broker, you should consider it your first and most important trade in the forex market. An investor entrusts their trading capital to the broker, with the intent of trading with that capital and then being able to withdraw it when they want to take their returns.

Different brokers will generally have their own unique way of dealing with transactions and executing orders. When determining which type of forex broker to use on the basis of their forex quotations, there are three main categories of brokers;

- No Dealing Desk Broker

- Market Makers

- Electronic Communications Network Brokers (ECN)

No dealing Desk Forex Broker (NDD)

The NDD forex broker does not have a dealing desk. This type of broker usually provides the best quotes. They get these quotes from a variety of forex quote providers.

Multiple quote providers usually present their best markets to the No Dealing Desk broker. The broker then executes the trades and fills orders for the clients. The No Dealing Desk broker usually charges a commission on the trades made or increase the bid/offer spread in order to make some profit on each trade.

It is important to also determine how much trading capital you will use. If your trading capital is small then your trade will be focused on micro-lots. On the other hand, if you have a high trading mini lots can be your starting point. A trading capital of at least $50,000 is required for a standard lot account. It is important to choose the appropriate broker and account type that will match your trading capital.

Different brokers offer various methods of depositing withdrawing your funds. You should, therefore, consider the ease of making deposits to your trading account that the broker is able to offer.

What does the broker offer?

If your focus is on day trading a no dealing desk would be ideal because you will be in a position to engage directly with the market without the need to forward your order through a trading desk. A trading desk may be more time consuming and has a tendency to result in re-quotes. The time delay occasioned by re-quotes can make you lose your trading opportunity.

It is important to ensure that your broker is duly registered and governed and operates within a properly established and regulated financial system. It is recommended that you work with brokers who are registered and governed by US, Japanese, Australian or UK regulations.

To ensure a good trading experience, select a responsive broker who will offer good customer service and ensure that your queries are resolved. To gauge the level of efficacy in customer service a particular broker has, you can start by opening a demo account with the brokers you have shortlisted and then send them online queries. This will enable you to monitor their responsiveness and efficacy of customer service.

- **Test out the Broker**

Once you have identified the brokers you are most interested in, you can then proceed to test them out. Your testing process should occur in the following sequence;

1. Open a demo account and take the time to understand the trading conditions indicated. Monitor whether your trades take time to execute, ideally they should execute immediately. Consider whether the spreads are tight and finally confirm the stability of the trading platform being used.

2. After testing the broker for a couple of weeks with the demo account and establishing that the broker meets the required standards, you can then proceed to open the live account. In the beginning use only part of the total trading capital that you intend to invest. For example, with a trading capital of $ 5,000 to deposit, you can start by depositing $500.

3. Once you have deposited into your trading account you can use your partial deposit to trade for a couple of weeks while monitoring the efficacy of the platform and the level of the customer support offered.

4. To gauge the ease of withdrawal that the broker offers, initiate a partial withdrawal from your trading account.

5. If you are satisfied with the first four steps, your due diligence is done and you can settle on the best broker and you can now proceed to trade fully.

How to Open a Forex Account

The characteristic market volatility and the availability of Once you have settled on the best broker for your needs, you will need a forex account. A foreign exchange account is the account into which you will deposit the trading capital that is required for trading in the forex market. Once you have opened the account and funded it with your initial investment or capital you are now ready to start trading.

Retail forex trading is usually executed through a brokerage, so you will need to identify the broker who best meets your requirements and open your trading account with them. When it comes to the choice of brokers you can elect to work with a broker who specializes in currency exchange markets or use the same broker you use to trade in the stock market since most will offer more than a specific type of trading i.e. a brokerage can offer both stock markets and forex trade markets

Once you have identified a broker, the account opening process requires that you provide your personal details to the broker. The personal details required include;

- Name and official address
- Contact details such as phone number and email.
- Currency in which you will operate your account
- Security details for your trading account such as password
- Age
- Citizenship
- Your Social Security Number

You will also need to provide your financial details and objectives including; your average yearly income, your overall financial status as well as your trading goals and intended objectives. After you have submitted all the pertinent personal details and information, the broker will require supporting documents such as ID and utility statements to help in verifying the information you submitted. After the broker has confirmed that the information you have provided is accurate, your trading account will be open for business and you can then deposit your initial investment and start trading.

Offshore trading accounts have also gained popularity due to favorable tax treatments in some locations and also in a bid to overcome overly restrictive regulations in the US such as the Foreign Account Tax Compliance Act. If you are based in the US, it is possible to start trading outside of US forex markets by simply opening an offshore trading account. Similar to the process when one is investing locally, the first step is to identify a broker.

While selecting a broker for an offshore trading account it's important to consider;

- Trading fees that will be applied to your offshore trades in terms of commissions and transaction fees.

- The minimum initial investment or capital that will be required to open and operate the offshore trading account.

- The standard of responsiveness of the broker to queries from the customer.

- The offshore broker should meet all regulatory standards as established by the regulatory bodies when it comes to forex trading this includes the CFTC (Commodity Futures Trading Commission) and the NFA (National Futures Association). To avoid compliance and regulatory glitches down the road, ensure that the broker you select is also compliant with their local laws and regulations

When opening the offshore trading account, documentation requirements will be more or less similar to the ones required when opening a local trading account. You may be required to submit a notarized copy of your passport and verification documents such as utility statements and financial statements that the offshore broker will use to confirm the accuracy of the information that you have provided. Normally client agreements detailing terms and conditions as well as client trading forms will need to be filled out and duly signed.

The minimum trading capital required to operate an offshore trading account will vary from broker to broker. Usually, brokers will offer flexible terms when it comes to minimum deposits into the offshore accounts with some accepting deposits as low as $ 100. There are also options to operate an IBC (International Business Corporation) which is an ideal option for traders looking to deposit significant sums into their trading accounts. For investors with a sizeable amount to invest ($100,000), opening an offshore international business corporation (IBC) or an offshore trust might be a more profitable option. An IBC offers the trader anonymity and allows them to trade without disclosing their personal details and information.

An IBC is one of the safest methods of operating an offshore trading account. When you open an IBC for offshore trading, you can bypass most of the normal reporting procedures and will further benefit from being able to recoup the initial costs through savings made on taxes.

While opening an offshore trading account is relatively easy, investors should ensure that they understand from the onset of the tax rates and procedures in the offshore location as well as legal and compliance standards expected.

Self-Empowerment and Useful Trading Tools

To achieve success in trading, self-empowerment is paramount as it augments the trader's decision-making skills by equipping him with the ability to utilize various trading tools that will make trading less challenging for beginners or novice traders. using a number of forex trading tools to complement their trading strategies.

Trading tools are indispensable in forex trading. Trading tools help to increase productivity and improve performance. Brokers supply traders with the most advanced trading platforms to help them gain the best possible trading experience. There are many powerful tools and features that you can use for enhanced trading experience.

Forex trading tools can be accessed through subscription services, or free of charge guides that are provided by multiple trading websites available online and accessible to anyone interested in increasing their trading knowledge and skills. Some brokers will also offer their clients access to trading tools that a trader can use to guide their trading moves. Multiple forex signal trading services can be easily accessed to obtain trading cues that can prove invaluable especially for beginners looking for helpful pointers and strategies.

Free Online Trading Tools

Fundamental analysis tools are useful and popular tools for traders that can be accessed freely online. This analysis includes tools such as economic news calendars. Economic news calendars are important analysis tools because policy and economic declarations, level of political stability in a country, employment levels are all factors that can impact on the values of a given currency meaning that keeping up with news and current events can enable you to predict the probable market trends and this will, in turn, enable you to make trades that are likely to move in the right direction.

Economic News Calendar Tool

The economic news calendar is a fundamental analysis tool. A news calendar tool gives traders information on expected market policies and pronouncements as well as policies and declarations made in the past that impacted the market performance and movement. Events such as expected policy declarations, major central bank statements, and upcoming trade agreements, elections, etc. are all included in the economic news calendar.

Information on expected economic policy declarations and releases is usually enumerated in the economic news calendar even two weeks prior to the announcements meaning that the trader gets sufficient forewarning, Availability of this information in advance gives the trader sufficient time to determine whether he should open new trades, close existing ones or hold his market positions.

Most forex brokers provide their clients with this tool though it can also be accessed through financial news websites. Depending on the significance of the economic declaration made, currency pairs can either move drastically as in cases where market volatility is created or experience minimal movement if the economic release is not drastic.

Financial News

Economic news is readily available and accessible through a myriad of sources. There are newspapers that are specifically dedicated to disseminating financial news and form an important information source for all traders in different markets including forex traders. In the US, The Wall Street Journal, Reuters are trusted and established sources of major financial new on both a local and international scale. Others such as the Financial Times and Bloomberg are also reliable sources that a trader can use to keep up to date with financial news from across the globe

When it comes to currency values, they will usually fluctuate based on factors such as interest rates declared by central banks. This means that financial news form a country's main financial institution can influence the value of a particular currency in the forex market. A country's political stability, geological events, and levels of employment are also important indicators with the potential to impact the value of the national currency.

Pip Calculator Tool

A pip can be defined as the lowest trading unit that can be associated with a currency pair. A pip calculator tool is used by a trader to establish the value of a pip by relating it to the position in the local or base currency. The pip value varies depending on the base and counter currencies in the currency pair that is being traded.

When using a pip calculator to determine the value of a pip, the forex trader will enter information on the currency pair being traded, the amount of currency in the trade, the leverage being used, and the total amount of the trade into the pip calculator. The pip calculator will then establish the pip value of each of the traders' positions. With the pip calculator tool, the forex trader is able to keep track of the worth of his various positions in the trading account.

Broker Spread Comparison Tool

It is normal practice for forex traders to evaluate the various dealing spreads of each broker before choosing a forex broker. When getting in and out of trades, the cost to the trader will be dependent on the size of the spread. Tight spreads offer the trader better exchange rates and therefore most forex traders tend to choose brokers who have tighter dealing spreads.

When the dealing spread is large, the cost of getting in and out of trades increasing significantly. This means that for forex traders intending to hold positions for a short time, their returns will be significantly diminished by the higher cost of trading. Essential wide dealing spreads are especially detrimental for traders such as scalpers who capitalize on short term trades to realize their profits.

Comparison websites that illustrate comparisons between brokers in terms of the size of the spread offered, enable a trader to view the comparisons based on the currency pair they want to trade when they want to trade and the length of the trade they intend to make. Using the spread comparison tool, a forex trader is able to determine which broker offers the best spreads for their particular needs and objectives. This tool is therefore vital when a trader is trying to identify the best broker to work with.

Forex Volatility Calculator

When selecting a currency pair to trade, it is important to consider pairs that do not have a limited range. The volatility calculator tool usually uses past exchange rate data to predict the probable volatility of a particular currency pair that is being traded. The forex volatility calculator effectively enables the trader to establish how a currency pairs' volatility and price compare to its past performance. A volatility calculator that can provide past volatility data on a currency pair broken down in terms of time frames such as weeks, months or years will generally be more accurate

Higher volatility creates greater opportunities in terms of possible margins and returns so the volatility calculator can enable a trader to trade with diminished risk exposure when dealing with volatile currency pairs.

MetaTrader 4

Most forex trading transactions are executed online. Trading technology is therefore due to this becoming increasingly advanced and traders can initiate trades within seconds via their preferred trading platform. MetaTrader 4 is a forex trading platform and has a high-level acceptance among traders as an effective trading tool in forex trade. It provides instrumental features that enable a forex trader to trade effectively and it is this comprehensive nature of this tool that has made it a popular tool in forex trading.

MetaTrader 4 enables traders to execute transactions in real-time by providing technical analysis data and market indicators to the trader. The integrated trading function that is built into the MetaTrader 4 platform means that a forex trader can trade currency pairs directly from the charts. When using this platform for trading you can use premade and customized indicators to direct your trades.

Another advantage to using the MetaTrader 4 is that it allows you to open and operate a demo account within the platform. With this demo account, you can test your strategies and evaluate them using the MetaTrader's testing module. This useful tool is accessed free of charge as an online download that is made available on the MetaTrader's developers' website.

Chapter 4: Financial Leverage

Leverage when it comes to financial markets refers to borrowing money that you can use to purchase assets that will generate returns for you in terms of profits. When you use leverage, you can reduce your initial investment since the leverage will multiply your capital. In essence, when your leverage is high your debt is equally high. When your leverage is low then the debt will also be minimal. Calculating leverage involves coming up with the ratio of debt/equity. For leverage to be beneficial to the trader, it needs to generate more returns or profits for the trader than the amount of interest that the trader will be required to pay on the debt.

Leverage is typically used in finance as a method of borrowing money for investment and then making use of the borrowed money to generate more returns due to the increased trading capital. Once you pay back the debt, the returns you remain with will be higher than what you would have made if you just traded with your own equity.

When it comes to trading, leverage means you can access a larger portion of the market with a smaller deposit than you would be able if you were using traditional investing. Leverage allows the trader to magnify his potential profits by giving him access to more money than he has in terms of trading capital.

What Is Financial Leverage?

Leverage is the ability to borrow and trade with more money than your available trading capital. Leverage allows a forex trader who has a limited initial investment to make money using the amount that is borrowed. In this way, a trader stands to make more profit since he has access to more funds that he can use to trade with. However, this leverage comes with an equal risk of multiplying your losses if the markets go against you. Access to leverage is one of the main reasons that investors choose to invest in forex trading.

The use of leverage is generally intended to;

- Increase the trader's asset base.

- Allow traders with limited capital to make more returns than their own equity would allow.

- Make savings in the form of tax deductions that are applicable for interest on leverage.

Leverage can be defined as either margin-based or real leverage. Forex trading allows traders to access high leverage whereby they can borrow substantial amounts to augment their asset base.

Margin-based leverage is determined by dividing the total transaction value by the amount of equity that you need.

In a scenario where you need to come up with a minimum of 1% of the transaction value, and your intended trade is USD 100,000, in this case, your leverage would be 100.1. This margin-based leverage is obtained when the total trade value of $ 100,000 is divided by the $1000 equity.

The same formula can be used to calculate margin-based leverage for different deposit requirements as per the below table.

Leverage	Deposit Required
400:1	0.25%
200:1	0.50%
100:1	1.00%
50:1	2.00%

Margin-based leverage does affect the risk level associated with a particular trade. A trader's profits or losses will not be influenced by the margin since any trading position can be entered into with more equity than what the margin stipulates. Therefore, the real indication of profit or loss on a leveraged trade will be determined using the real leverage and not the margin-based leverage.

Real Leverage is calculated using the Total Value of Transaction / Total Trading Capital. In effect to calculate real leverage, the total value of transactions is divided by the trading capital. For instance, your real leverage will be 10 times if you trade $ 100,000 with a capital of $ 10,000.

Real leverage will typically differ from margin-based leverage since traders will not commit their entire trading capital as equity in each trade. In forex trading, traders can access high amounts of leverage to trade with, Traders can access up to 100 times of their capital in leverage and this serves to increase the potential returns they are likely to make.

When a trading account is managed effectively the risks that come with leverage will also be diminished. When a trader is able to effectively manage their risks, they can effectively make use of leverage to gain access to more trades and therefore make more profits. Liquid markets enable a trader to exit and enter trades quickly and this liquidity is part of the reason that leverage works well in the foreign exchange trade.

Minimal price movements yield higher profits for the trader if the trader has access to leverage. You are likely to make more money if you can trader with $100,000 in leverage than if you just trade with your own equity, let's say $ 1,000. The leverage multiplies the profit factor making substantial impacts on potential profits and returns.

Advantages of Financial Leverage

Increased Profit

Traders get into forex trading with their main aim being to make profits on their investments. Leverage effectively increases the size of the profits you stand to make in any particular trade where leverage is applied. By increasing your asset base, leverage gives you more money to work with meaning you can put more on a trade and get more out of it. From a starting capital of just $ 1000, leverage can give you access to up to $100,000 which is a significant difference in terms of the profits you can realize even from small market movements.

Leverage is a means for the trader to use more money on his trades without necessary tying up all of their trading capital. This means you can make more profit by risking more but still remaining with part of your initial investment. In effect, leverage simply works by increasing your asset base and multiplying your potential profits.

Trading Capital Efficiency

Your trading capital is an asset with the ability to generate returns or profit. When you can utilize this asset properly and realize more returns per trade by using leverage, it means that the trading capital is used more efficiently. Leverage allows you to make more money within shorter periods of time and this will allow you to re-invest your trading capital more times which will ultimately increase your returns. Leverage makes a significant impact on capital efficiency by ensuring greater profits in the short-term. When your trading capital is tied up over long periods of time, it diminishes your ability to reinvest meaning that the amount of money you are able to generate from your capital will be limited leverage can help you avoid this situation.

Leverage Mitigates Against Low Volatility

Leverage mitigates against the diminished profit margins that are characteristic of markets with minimal volatility. When price fluctuations are big, this volatility creates the opportunity for a trader to make more money. Leverage by giving you access to more funds enables you to make good returns even when market volatility is low by increasing the multiplication factor of the returns.

Leverage enables a forex trader to make money even when market movements are minimal so that you can still make decent profits when the market volatility is low. This is important to a trader because markets tend to have low volatility unless there are unexpected movements that cause drastic changes in the markets. This means that if you can only make a profit when the market volatility is high, your chances of profitability will be limited to the few periods when the markets become highly volatile. Volatile trades are often those that deliver the greatest degrees of profit because of the.

Risks of Financial Leverage and How to Manage Them

The magnifying effect of leverage on your asset base applies to both the potential for profits and the potential for risks. In the same way, it can magnify your profits, it can also magnify losses. Understanding how leverage can impact on your portfolio is the first step towards managing the risks posed by financial leverage.

Heavier Losses

Leverage paves the way for heavier losses. The effect of leverage on trade is that it gives you more money to work with. The more money you are working with, the more money you stand to lose if the trade goes against you. Simply put if you commit $1000 to trade then you can only lose that much, however, if you commit $100,000, then in case of a loss that is the amount you stand to lose.

Leverage is a Liability

Borrowing money is essentially acquiring a liability. The amount borrowed must be paid back, and this cost will also include the interest that accrues on the principal amount. Leverage is a debt that a trader takes on to multiply their stake. This debt can be beneficial in a scenario where your profits on a particular trade are enough to cover the amount borrowed and leave you with some profits or it can be detrimental when you lose money on a trade and you have to cover the cost of the debt. When you leverage a trade, it means that you have to meet the cost of the leverage as well as generate profit for yourself. In essence, leverage is a liability that requires you to make more returns to remain profitable.

Interest

In any financial transaction where money is borrowed for use in purchasing of an asset, the principal amount accrues interest that needs to be paid back with the initial amount that was borrowed. When it comes to leverage interest must be paid on the principle and this can cause losses to the trader especially if the leveraged trade did not realize sufficient returns. This interest costs can add up and in effect create a disincentive for holding exposure long term.

Managing the Risks of Financial Leverage

When it comes to risk management, the ability to effectively limit the risk exposure that comes with leverage is one of the key considerations for any trader who wants to make money. For any forex trader who wants his investment to yield returns, risk management should be the top priority. Managing risks effectively is the primary determinant of the ability to succeed in forex trading. Without proper risk management, an investor stands the risk of losing his trading capital and going out of business.

Avoid over-leveraging. Over leveraging is effectively taking on leveraged positions at sizes your trading account can't handle. Whether it's across one trade or multiple trades your total exposure to leveraged risk should not put you in a position where you face possible margin call or capital insolvency if things go bad.

To avoid falling into the over-leveraging trap, consider applying small amounts of leverage per trade. When you do this, you can diminish the risk of losing a lot of money if a particular trade does not go as expected. By risking fewer amounts in terms of leverage, you ultimately limit your exposure to loses. However, the risks that come with leverage should not put you off taking advantage of this opportunity when engaging in forex trading. You can easily reap the benefits of leverage by settling on a leverage amount that is suitable for you and will be manageable for your trading account. you can opt to use lower leverage amounts as you start trading until you get more experienced and better at winning trades.

The basic points to use to effectively manage risks of financial leverage are:
- Applying trailing stops to your trades
- Making small trades.
- Restricting the capital used per trade.

Take a conservative approach to manage your trading capital. Remember that trading is as much about prudence as it is about risk. To trade successfully in the forex market, you need to be able to strike the best balance between prudence and risk in order to get the most from your trading activity.

Chapter 5: Basics of Technical Analysis

There are many risks in forex trading and any investor venturing into this field should arm themselves with the tools for minimizing risk and exposure when trading. Technical analysis provides a trader with the knowledge and skills that he requires to execute his strategies effectively and increases the probability of getting good returns on their investment.

When making decisions in forex trading it is important to have data and information that can guide you in knowing the best entry and exit points into a trade, which currency pairs are best for your purposes and even how long you should hold a position. Analysis in the forex markets is done using either technical analysis tools or fundamental analysis tools.

Technical analysis in forex trading refers to the study of market fluctuations and price movements that occur in the forex market. Traders make use of historical chart patterns and indicators to predict future trends in the market. Technical analysis is the visual representation of the past as well as the present performance of a market. It allows the trader to use this information in the form of price action, patterns, and indicators to predict future trends before entering a forex trade. Technical analysis basically involves the interpretation of trends and patterns from charts. By making use of historic data on past prices and market movements, traders can use this data to draw conclusions on expected trends and market direction thereby effectively identifying trading opportunities based on the common patterns that show up in the past data. Traders can use the various indicators from the analysis to establish the best entry and exit points for trades in order to maximize the potential of good risk-reward ratios.

Technical analysis is used to study the price patterns on a particular asset. When traders are carrying out technical analysis they will focus on;

1. **Technical Analysis Chart Patterns**

   Technicians use drawing tools such as horizontal lines, trend lines and Fibonacci levels to identify well-known classical chart patterns such as symmetrical triangle formations and consolidation patterns. These patterns indicate the strength and weaknesses of buyers and sellers in the market.

2. **Technical Analysis Candle Patterns**

   In this type of analysis, technicians use candle charts for the analysis. Candle charts usually illustrate data on price changes over particular periods of time in a bid to identify the behavior of buyers and sellers within a short period of time.

3. **Technical Analysis Indicators**

   In this analysis, technicians use price action indicators to help in understanding the market condition. Most indicators will give signals on when the market is overbought or oversold. Other indicators provide clues on the rising and falling momentum.

The History of Technical Analysis

Technical analysis of the financial markets has existed since the establishment of trading markets that are dictated by market forces that depend on the demand for a particular product in relation to the available supply of the product in question. Historical data on technical analysis date back to the 17th. In this century history records show that Dutch merchants employed a level of technical analysis to their trading. By the 18th century, the technical analysis had started spreading to other parts of the world.

Charles Dow the founder and editor of The Wall Street Journal brought technical analysis to traders in the 19th century. Along with Charles Dow, there were other individuals credited with the growth of technical analysis as part of market analysis in forex trading.

The Elliot Wave theory was founded by Ralph Elliot in the early 1920s. With his discovery that seemed to indicate a cyclic movement in stock markets, Ralph Willison was able to establish the wave theory. He was able to draw correlations between the general market feeling and the direction the markets took as a result. He also found that external factors were capable of influencing market trends in the markets.

The patterns that developed in response to the mass psychology prevalent at any given time were found to occur in wave-like patterns. This finding aligned with the Dow theory that related the stock prices to wave-like movements. Going by the fractal nature of these patterns, Ralph Elliot was able to analyze the markets on a deeper level.

Fractal patterns are repetitive and once Elliott found these patterns in the market, he was able to develop a means of predicting the market. Other pioneers in the field include William Delbert Gann who founded the Gann angle theory and Richard Demille Wyckoff. Richard Demille theorized that the past patterns observed in markets should be analyzed as a single entity.

Initially, most of the technical analysis was done using charts. However, the current digital era has enabled statistical computation of vast amounts of data.

Advantages of Technical Analysis:
- Forex technical analysis requires just a few basic tools which are available to the trader free of charge on platforms such as MetaTrader.

- Forex technical analysis can be used to determine the best points of entry and exit from the market.

- There are a wide variety of readily available technical analysis tools and indicators that are useful in identifying trading setups.

- Can be applied to any market using any timeframe

- Technical analysis can be used as a standalone method

Disadvantages of Technical Analysis:
- Forex technical analysis is widely used and can, therefore result in abrupt market movements when many traders come to the same conclusions.

- In some markets, the efficacy of technical analysis requires that it be combined with fundamental analysis.

Fundamental Analysis

Financial markets are impacted and influenced by factors such as interest rates, political and policy declarations, financial and the overall business stability in a country and a host of other factors. By studying all these factors, traders can determine how they impact market trends by influencing the movement of assets in either an upward or downward trajectory. The analysis of current events, financial news and policy releases and their effect on the markets is referred to as fundamental analysis.

The study of financial data such as inflation reports, employment levels, etc. or company news and earnings to identify the trend of the market and possible turning points of a particular market is what makes up fundamental analysis. When the financial stability of a country is good and the economy is vibrant, the currency of that country is bound to strengthen and increase in value, on the other hand, a poor financial outlook and poor business environment is likely to result in the depreciation of a currency. In effect, these are the factors that fundamental analysis uses in enabling traders to predict outcomes in the trading markets.

Economic Calendar

An economic calendar is used in fundamental analysis. It typically shows upcoming events across the globe. Items indicated on the economic calendar are usually ranked in order of importance that is either low, medium or high.

The forex calendar can be used to see which events could subtly shift markets or significantly shake up the financial markets. The FX calendar can be customized to keep track of the specific data you're interested in.

Advantages of Fundamental Analysis:
- Fundamental analysis can help you understand the reason behind a market movement.

- A trader can use fundamental analysis to complement other types of analysis that he uses for predicting the expected long-term trends.

Disadvantages of Fundamental Analysis:
- There are so many fundamental analysis tools that can lead to conflicting conclusions and data.

- Fundamental analysis is time-consuming because it requires constant keeping track of all the different news and economic pronouncements.

- It takes longer to master the impact of different economic data such as inflation reports and interest rates on markets.

Technical vs fundamental analysis comparison

	Technical Analysis	**Fundamental Analysis**
Definition	Forecast price movements using chart patterns	Economic data used to establish value
Data used	Price action (charts)	Inflation, GDP, interest rates, etc.
Timeline	Short, medium and long term	Medium and long term
Skills	Chart analysis	Economics & statistical analysis

It is common for traders to use technical analysis in combination with some fundamental analysis or sentiment. While the identification of market trends falls under the province of technical analysis, these trends are brought about by fundamental factors making fundamental analysis an important tool in forex trading.

Tools for Analysis

When analyzing markets, there are various mechanisms that can be used. These include;
1. Technical Analysis Charts
2. Technical Analysis Chart Patterns
3. Technical Analysis Candlestick Patterns
4. Technical Analysis Indicators

Technical Analysis Charts

Charts are key to technical analysis because the most important measure of a market's past and current performance is the price itself. when delving into analyzing the potential of a particular trade the starting point is usually the past and current performance of the market. Price action can be represented on a chart as this is the clearest indication of what the price is doing.

Charts are used to determine the overall trend. Charts indicate whether there's an upward or downward trend, in the long term or short term and also identify range-bound conditions. The most common types of charts employed in forex markets are;

- Bar charts
- Line charts
- Candlestick charts

In a bar or candlestick chart, each period will give the technical analyst information on the price. This data will include where the price opened from, the high or low of the period as well as the close.

Candlestick analysis is useful because the patterns and relationships within them can assist in making forecasts about the future direction of the price.

Once a trader has mastered the basics of charting, they can then make use of indicators to assist in determining the trend.

Line Charts

A line chart displays closing prices and only. Each closing price is linked to the previous closing price to make a continuous line that is easy to follow.

Line charts are often used for television, newspapers and many web pages because they are simple and easy to understand. Line charts provide less information than the candlestick or bar charts. Line charts provide a simplistic market view.

A sample line chart is illustrated below

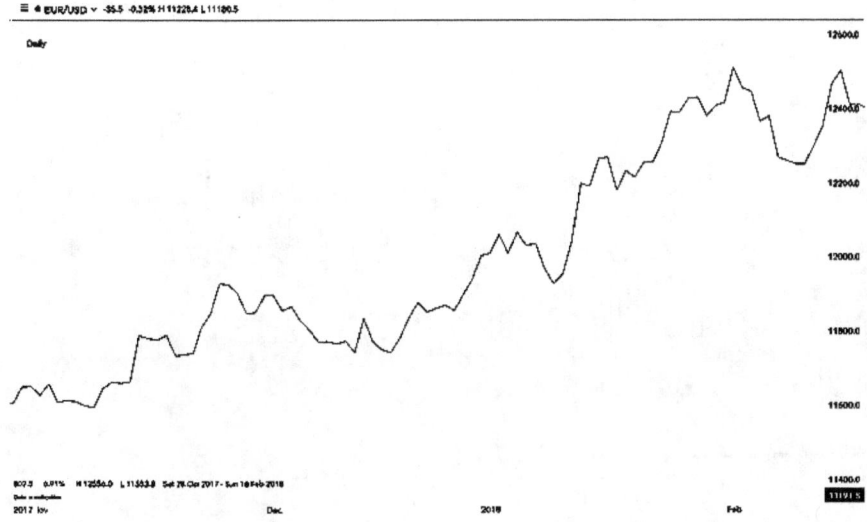

Bar Charts

A bar chart is used to illustrate the high, low, open and closing prices for particular trade durations. In the chart, the high and low prices are plotted by the vertical line. The dash to the left represents the opening price while dash to the right signals the closing price. A trader is able to determine the market sentiment for a particular period by identifying whether a bar closes up (green) or down (red),) for that period.
A sample bar chart is illustrated below

Candlestick Charts

A candlestick chart typically shows the top and bottom prices, as well as the opening and final prices for each period designated for the chart. The "body" of each candlestick represents the opening and closing prices while the wicks" display the high and low prices for each period.

A sample candlestick chart is illustrated below.

The candlestick chart is the most popular type of chart used in forex technical analysis since it provides the trader with more information while remaining easy to view and analyze.

Technical Analysis Indicators

Technical analysis indicators are used by technical traders to identify opportunities in the market. Indicators usually assist traders in analyzing the market, validating trade setups and determining entry points.

Most traders use of volume and priced-based indicators. These two types of indicators assist in identifying where the levels of support and resistance are. A trader can view the price or any other indicator using multiple time frame analysis. The timeline can range from a day to a month.

Popular indicators for technical analysis include:
- Moving Averages
- The RSI index
- The MACD

The MACD as well as the moving averages indicators aid in the understanding of market trends while the RSI (Relative Strength Index) is typically used to determine possible entry and exit points.

Applying Forex Market Analysis

A trader needs to understand how to apply market analysis to his trading plan. The following steps outline how to maximize the impact of market analysis on your trades.

1. Understand the Drivers

Successful forex trading requires a trader to be able to identify what is prompting the changes in the market trends and how these prompts relate to and influence the market. For example, market recovery could be prompted by investors predicting a financial upswing which would mean that earnings would be likely to increase and that the currency value would likely strengthen in the future as a result. In such a case the traders might opt to buy in while the asset is expected to rise so that they can sell when the price reaches a high.

2. Chart the Indexes

To understand the market movements of particular currency pairs, a trader can chart indexes for each currency and observe it over an extended duration. These indexes can help traders determine whether currency pairs are positively and negatively correlated. The type of correlation will ultimately impact the profit or loss potential of a trade.

3. Determine if there are Conformities in Other Markets

Charting other securities and their trends over the same duration can give an indication of a possible change in the market trend. When we can determine the possibility of a market turn, it makes it possible to advantage of the situation by making a trade that is likely to benefit from the market change.

4. Time the Trades

The duration of your trades should be directed by the possibility of market turns on a particular security. When you identify possible turning points, you can opt for a shorter trade to minimize your risk exposure by avoiding unexpected changes in prices.

Using indicators to guide your trading plan enables you to make sound informed decisions that will increase your chances of trading successfully in the forex market. Prior preparation and adequate planning are important strategies that every trader should employ when trading.

Chapter 6: Strategies for Beginners

Market fluctuations are an inevitable part of forex trading. These unexpected changes can pose risks for both novice traders and experienced traders and require a trading plan in order to execute successful trades. It is easy to fall into the school of thought that equates success in trading to using complex strategies. More often than not more straight forward strategies are easier to adopt, follow and more effective. Whichever strategy you opt to use in your trading there are basic elements that every beginner should consider before they start trading. These are;

- **Trading capital management** – You need to decide on the amount of initial investment you want to begin trading with. This will also involve setting a guideline on the amount that you can use per trade.
- **Time management** – Forex trading requires commitment in terms of time that you will spend analyzing and predicting market trends so that you can use the information to guide your trades. Successful trading cannot be accomplished without proper planning or preparation both of which demand that you put some fair amount of time into your trading.
- **Do not over trade** – While you're getting the hang of things in the forex market, it is wise to limit the number of trades that you execute. Entering into multiple trades per day is bound to deplete your capital without any gains. Starting small helps you manage your capital and get better at trading without unnecessary risks. You can set a limit on the number of trades you execute in a day regardless of whether the previous trades win or lose.
- **Learning** – Staying informed and being able to identify market indicators will improve your chances of success. Familiarizing yourself with various analysis platforms will empower you to trade more profitably.

- **Consistency** – Sticking to your trading plan will help you keep emotions at bay. The main strategy should be to stay within your strategy, work within your budget and not let overconfidence or anxiety distract you from the plan.
- **Patience** – Markets changes are inevitable parts of the forex trade. Ensure that you exercise patience and avoid making rash decisions.

As a beginner in forex trading, it is also important for you to consider three essential components that will enable you to profit even when market movements are marginal. These components are:

1. **Liquidity** – The liquidity of a particular trade will make entering and exiting trades easy and will not be costly for you.

2. **Volatility** – Volatility typically impacts on the potential profit or loss you stand to make on a trade

3. **Volume** –High trading volume usually indicates that there is a significant interest in the trade can be an indicator of a price movement either upwards or downwards.

The most successful traders enhance their trading skills through consistent practice and self-discipline. Self-analysis is a useful tool that you can use to determine what drives your trades. Some of the basic strategies to consider for any investor starting out in the foreign exchange market are;

Follow the Trend

When you are just getting started in forex trading being able to follow the general market movements will help you in making profitable trades. When you establish the direction of the trend, then the trades you enter should be in the general direction of the trend. Market direction can be extended or limited to a short duration so the expected length of the trend should guide you on whether to adopt a long term or short term trading plan. Based on the time frame selected, you can then determine the type of charts to use.

Moving Averages

Moving averages provide buy and sell signals to the trader. They will help you understand the current market trends. You can obtain buy and sell indicators using moving averages by plotting different means on the same chart and observing the points at which they cross.

Oscillators

Oscillators help us to identify the markets that have either been overbought or oversold. Oscillators will guide you on the best entry point into a market. The Relative Strength Index (RSI) and the stochastic oscillators are popular among forex traders. They vary on a scale ranging from 0 to 100. A Relative Strength Index that is more than 70, will indicate that the market has been overbought while when the index is below 30 it is indicative that there is no overbooking.

A change in the market trend will be signaled by a divergence where the signal from the oscillators different from the price direction.

The ADX Index

The Average Directional Movement Index can be used to establish whether or not a market trend is strong. When the ADX index exceeds 25, the implication that the trend is strong. The ADX index does not indicate in which direction the trend is moving.

Retracements and Corrections

When a trade corrects either up or down it propagates the past market trend. Using a trend percentage, you can determine the level of the correction in a particular market. In the forex markets, investors tend to follow the Fibonacci retracements which are 38% and 62 %.

Buy Low and Sell High

Profit is primarily obtained when you can dispose of an asset at a greater price than what you paid for it. Buying low and selling high can be a very effective strategy in forex trading because it allows you to spend less while making more.

The problem with this strategy is knowing when you are at a low and when you are at a high. The price can fall significantly and look like a good opportunity to buy but as soon as you enter a trade, the price falls further and you make a loss. This can be very frustrating. This can put you in a cycle where you keep on buying as the price continues to fall meaning that you will then make multiple substantial losses.

To effectively apply the strategy of buy low and sell high, you need to avoid buying something that is still falling. There are three main strategies that can reduce the risks that come with a buy high and sell a low model of trade. These indicators include pivot lines that establish resistance levels and support levels and the Relative Strength Index which signal market direction. The assumption that "the price can't go any lower", can cause you to lose money on bad trades by giving you a false sense of the market.

Using the following indicators will prove useful in gauging the best exit and entry points on a trade.

Pivot Lines

When it comes to predicting possible support and resistance levels to mitigate risks and increase potential returns, pivot lines are an efficient indicator. You can find an entry point into a trade by identifying a high low or an exit point by identifying a low high by using pivot lines.

When your trading is not guided by limits, your risk exposure increases and you are more likely to lose on your trades. Support and resistance levels provide you with a safeguard by giving you an indicator of the range you need to operate within. A trade moving in the right direction and making you money can go bad if you do not exit the market at the right point.

RSI

The Relative Strength Index is an indicator of the strength of the market direction. Traders are able to identify strong entries that favor the RSI bias. Adding a trending line to the RSI is a simple but effective way to establish the directional bias on the Relative Strength Index.

Trendlines

Depending on the market movement, a trader can determine the best buying opportunities that will net him the best possible returns. The best buying opportunities are usually present when the market is in a rising trajectory while the best time to buy is when there is a downward trajectory in the market movement.

Trendlines are a useful indicator when trying to pinpoint a better probability entry or exit point

Stop Loss

Market fluctuations and volatility in the foreign exchange market are a constant risk factor for investors in the currency exchange market. Mechanisms such as Stop Loss can be used by traders to prevent trades from incurring high losses that can be occasioned by fluctuations in the market and market volatility.

Rapid market movements characteristic of the forex trading market lead to rapid changes in especially in situations when trends change directions. In these cases, a stop-loss mechanism can be used to close a trade at the indicated final level at which you can accept a loss. By setting a final level at which you can accept loss you in effect minimize the risk exposure occasioned by volatile market changes.

When choosing an effective and appropriate stop-loss limit, you should keep the following factors in mind;

- The length of the trade, longer trades are generally riskier.
- The target price
- The size of your account and current balance.
- The number of open positions you have.
- The size of your order and whether it matches your, account balance and time frame.
- The general market sentiment at the time of entering the trade (for instance, is it volatile, awaiting news or other external factors?)
- The time frame available before the market closes. (for instance, is it almost weekend?)

When placing Stop loss limits, you can apply the following strategies;

Static Stops

This type of limit involves using fixed prices as a stop level. The Static stop remains in place for the duration of the trade until the target price or reached or the stop limit is reached. Using a static stop mechanism This type of stop mechanism is straightforward, it enables forex traders to stick to a minimum one-to-one risk-to-reward ratio.

Trailing Stops

In these types of stops, changes can be made to the limit price specified depending on the direction in which the trade is moving. Trading stops are not fixed to a particular price and provide a flexible mechanism that can be adjusted to suit the market direction if it presents an opportunity for the trader to make better returns on his trade.

Fixed Trailing Stops

In these kinds of stops, the limits set will be changed incrementally as the trade moves in a direction that is profitable to the trader. You can, for instance, put a trailing stop that changes after every 15 pips gained in the trade. This process continues until either the stop level is hit or the trader manually closes the trade.

Take Profit

A trader can implement a limit that effectively exits a trade when a predetermined profit level is attained. This type of limit order will help in managing risks by closing the trade once you attain the intended profit level. This is useful because a good trade can turn bad if a change in the market direction occurs unexpectedly and reverses the course of the market

A take profit order is ideal for short term trades. Pivot points or average true range are used when a trader is trying to establish the right profit limit to use for his trade. Without a set profit limit for trades, it may be difficult to have a good understanding of the best time to exit the trade. Take profit orders may not be ideal for long term traders because they may exit a trade too early and lose out on any further gains.

Usually, a trader will benefit when the take profit limit is higher than the entry price and when it facilitates an exit from the market before the prices start to fall, meaning that the trader is able to exit at the highest point possible. Indicators are used in predicting possible market trends.

Take-profit order limits are mostly determined using analysis of charts or studying the resistance and support limits in a particular market. A trader can also identify the best profit levels to set limits by referring to capital management techniques that will guide him in setting limits that do not carry considerable risks that could jeopardize his trades.

When using a take-profit order as a risk management tool, it is also possible to use a stop-loss order simultaneously such that your profit limit is regulated by a take profit order while your loss is regulated by a stop-loss limit. This means that whether a market is rising or falling you will have a limit on each side to keep your trades in check.

Best Currencies to Follow

All trade in the forex market involves the sale of one currency which is the base currency and the purchase of another which is the counter currency. This global market effectively facilitates international transactions by allowing the conversion of one currency to another. The forex market is global and as such operates throughout the 24 hours of a day.

It is common for new traders in the forex market to become daunted by the choice of currency pairs that are available for trading in the foreign exchange market. With so many currency options available to traders, it can be difficult identifying the best pairs to trade in and which pairs are risky for your investment. For every trader that wants to make money in forex, understanding the different currency pairs and knowing which ones will best fit into your trading plan is imperative.

Forex trade is built around the buying of one currency and the selling of another. The two currencies that are traded make up the currency pair. To make successful trades, a trader needs to have an understanding of how the two currencies in the pair compare to each other. The relationship between the two currencies to be traded will form the basis of your decision of whether the two will be a profitable trade or not.

When considering currency pairs, pay attention to the stability of the currency in question. Currencies that are susceptible to high rates of fluctuations will make your trades riskier while stable currencies are more likely to have predictable market trends. Currencies, where the financial and business sectors are relatively stable, are therefore good options for traders starting out in forex.

Working with currencies from countries with stable economies such as Switzerland, Canada, Australia or the United States is usually a safer bet for traders due to their high level of liquidity and because there is a level of security that comes with trading in stable currency pairs.

The currency pairs that are highly traded in the forex markets are;

- British Pound – US Dollar
- Euro – US Dollar
- US dollar – Japanese Yen
- Australian Dollar – US Dollar
- US Dollar – Swiss Franc
- US Dollar – Canadian Dollar

In currency pairs where trade volumes between the different countries keep changing, the level of volatility is high which means that prices are prone to fluctuations.

EUR/USD (Euro – US Dollar)

This currency pair is the most popular in forex trading. The Euro – Us dollar pair makes up 27% of the trading volume in the forex market. Due to the low volatility of this currency pair, price fluctuations are usually low and therefore trading this pair carries a minimal risk for the trader. This minimal risk makes it the best currency pair to trade for someone looking for low-risk trades.

Another advantage of trading in this currency pair is that there is a wealth of information available on it hence analysis its trends should much easier than when working with pairs that are not commonly traded. The high trade volumes of this pair also mean that it has the highest liquidity.

USDJPY at 13%, then followed by the GBPUSD at 12% of the total forex trading volume

GBP/USD (British Pound – US Dollar)

The profitable pips and possible large jumps in prices have made this currency popular among forex traders. The GBP/USD pair can be classified as a volatile currency pair. This volatility translates into higher returns for traders who trade in this pair if the market moves as they had predicted. This pair makes up 12% of the total trading volume in the forex markets. Despite its popularity, it is a risky pair due to its volatility.

USD/JPY (US dollar – Japanese Yen)

The USD/JPY currency pair is also popular in forex trading because it is generally a stable currency pair that is not susceptible to frequent volatility. It, therefore, presents a stable option for traders looking to trade a pair that has a fairly predictable market movement and that does not carry too much risk in terms of losses.

Compare Currencies

As a general rule of thumb for profitable forex trading, when it comes to a spread 3 pips or lower are ideal. Currency pairs with a high spread will have a proportionately high risk. In a currency with a spread in excess of 6 pips, there is a greater risk of a losing trade.

Currency pairs that are not paired with the U.S. dollar are referred to as crosses. They include;

- Euro -Japanese yen
- Australian dollar - Japanese yen
- British pound - Japanese yen
- Euro - Australian dollar
- Euro - British pound

Currency pairs that consist of currencies from smaller economies are referred to as exotic currency pairs. These include currency pairs such as; Euro vs. the Turkish lira or U.S. dollar vs. the South African rand. Since these types of pairs are not commonly traded their level of liquidity is low and their trading volume in the forex market is also pretty low.

Chapter 7: Manage Your Emotions with Trading Psychology

> *The key to trading success is emotional discipline. If intelligence were the key, there would be a lot more people making money trading*
>
> Victor Sperandeo

Emotions are at the core of the human experience. Our first line knee jerk reactions to experiences, people and phenomena are always on an emotional level. We can therefore not ignore the impact that emotions have on our ability to successfully navigate through life in terms of relationships, career, and business.

Emotional intelligence is now widely recognized as an instrumental factor for success both in the workplace and personal levels. The ability to not only recognize but also manage your emotions will go a long way in ensuring that the decisions you make are based on logic and not on emotional highs and lows.

A key tenement of emotional intelligence is self-awareness. Self-awareness requires you to be aware of what you are feeling and also identify the trigger or triggers that make you feel a particular aware. To be self-aware you will need to practice self-analysis through reflection to identify the behavioral tendencies that you develop based on your emotional weather. While it may sound like a straight forward concept, emotional reactions occur on a subconscious level and you would be surprised at how many times we make emotion-driven decisions without even being aware of it.

The Basics of Trading Psychology

The ability to control emotions while trading can make the difference between success and failure in forex trading. Your mental state has a significant impact on the decisions that you make. This is especially true for a new trader in the forex market. Emotions can lead to greed, where you might end up taking unnecessary risks and ignoring your trading plan in order to make a quick buck.

Some of the most common emotions traders experience include fear, nervousness, excitement, greed, and overconfidence.

Fear/Nervousness

Fear is a natural human emotion especially when we perceive a situation that could be damaging to either ourselves or our best interests. This holds for investors in different fields including foreign exchange traders. A common cause of fear in trading is when a trader has put too much of their capital on a trade or made a move on a volatile market magnifying their risk exposure and increasing the probability of losses.

Over-leveraging yourself, lack of a solid trading plan and improper execution of trading strategies can cause the trader experience fear of losing their trading capital and ending up in losses.

Greed/Overconfidence

Greed can be a result of impatience where a trader wants to realize huge returns within a short period of time or when a trader on a profitable streak becomes overconfident and tries to go for more and more profits. If you find yourself developing a tendency of preferring only trades that promise big returns you may be letting greed guide your trading.

Typical examples of greed in forex trading include;
- 'Doubling down' on losing trades
- Adding capital to winning positions
- Over-leveraging

Greed will often result in traders placing trades they otherwise would never have thought of executing. In addition, greed will ultimately pose a threat to your trading capital and account. Doubling down on losing trades, adding too much capital to winning positions, and over-leveraging can quickly result in a margin call or can deplete your trading capital.

While it is natural to want to make the most out of your investments if you find yourself constantly throwing caution to the wind and engaging in high-risk trades for a quick pay off you may be letting greed influence your trading experience and will likely end up incurring losses due to poor risk management.

Overconfidence can also result in poor decision making when trading. Markets can change rapidly due to any number of factors and a good streak can turn on a dime and that profits can rapidly turn to loss if you do not have effective stop and take profit mechanisms in place. Sloppy trading as a result of overconfidence can end a strong run.

Conviction/Excitement

Not all emotions can be classified as 'bad' for trading. Trading like any other venture requires an individual to have sufficient levels of self-motivation and drive to keep them going. Conviction and excitement are key emotions that a trader can feed off to inspire their trading plans and strategies.

Conviction is the final piece of any good trade, and if you do not have some level of excitement or conviction in the trades you are making then there is a good chance you are not in the right trade for you.

While good trades can also result in losses just like bad trades, the principle to work with is that you should be winning or losing on good trades.

Winning and Losing Mindsets in Trading

A successful trader realizes that success will stem from a winning mindset. The mindset of a successful trader simply deals with the experience of losses and failures differently. To develop a successful forex trading mindset, it is important to deal with both profits and losses in such a way that they do not cause you to deviate from your trading plan and strategies.

A losing mindset will be characterized by;

- Lack of a trading plan. Trading without a solid plan is akin to gambling. A plan helps in mapping out your trading strategies and in avoiding poor decision making.
- Trading based on greed. We all want to make money, but letting greed drive your trading will cause more losses than profits.
- Overleveraging. It is tempting to over-leverage in an attempt to maximize on returns, but you should remember that leverage multiplies your risk factor in much the same it does your profit.

Steps to Develop a Winning Mindset

1. Have Realistic Expectations

While forex trading can be lucrative, approaching it with a get-rich-quick mentality will decrease your chances of successful trading. Poor risk management in an attempt to make a lot of money in a short period of time is almost always a self-defeating strategy.

2. Trade with Money You Do Not Need to Live

When investing in any venture, it is wise to use money that you do not require for day to day living expenses. Trading capital should come from your disposable income. Trading with money that you need to live on will lead to severe emotional pressure which will, in turn, impact your trading decisions and is likely to result in losses.

3. Develop Patience

Successful traders understand the power of patience. When you are patient you will be able to stick with your trading plan and will not allow emotions such as greed or anxiety to influence your trading plan.

4. Understand That Trades Are Not Inter-Dependent

It is easy to be tempted to over trade after a losing trade or after a winning trade. This is because you will be trying to make up for lost money or trying to capitalize on a winning streak. In both these cases, you will have let the outcome of your past trade influence the next one. This is not a good trading strategy. Your last trade should have no impact on the next trade.

Every trade should be in keeping with your trading plan and strategy and not a reaction to your last trade. For example, if you just had three consecutive winning trades, do not risk an unusual amount on the next trade assuming that the fourth trade will be a success because the first three were successes. Similarly, losing a particular trade should not be taken as an indicator that you are on a losing streak. When you start basing your trades on your past trades then you are operating on emotion rather than a logical trading plan.

5. Have a Trading Plan

It is commonly said that failing to plan, is planning to fail. Forex trading is not exempt from this rule. Like any other venture, you should go into trading with clear goals and objectives as well as a road map on how to achieve them.

A trading plan will keep you on track and help you avoid making emotional and rash decisions. A trading plan does not need to be complicated to be effective, simply writing a plan of what your objectives for the next week or trading session are will keep you on track while making your trades.

Day Trading or Long-Term Trading?

Timing is a crucial factor in forex trading and results in different categories of trading depending on the length of the trades that are made. These categories of trading include;

- Day trading
- Long term trading
- Swing trading

Day trading

Day trading is characterized by entering and exiting a trade position at a very fast rate. This means that volume and liquidity are important factors in day trading. Currency pairs with a small daily range or volume make an ideal market for a day trader. Forex day traders typically focus on the events that cause short-term forex market moves. This means that trading the news is a prevalent technique in day trading.

Day traders will typically trade based on the information they acquire from economic news releases. These economic releases cause significant moves in the forex market when they are met or exceeded and these moves, in turn, generate profits for day traders. The price volatility of a particular currency and its average daily range is an important element in day trading.

The allure of fast and quick money that is characteristic of day trading is what attracts most beginners to this type of forex trading. Proficient scalpers are able to make quick money even though they take more risks. The limited timeframe of the short term trades can effectively limit your risk exposure in the market since you are trading for a limited period.

Day trading is a high pressure and high-stress environment that can prove challenging for beginners because they have a limited window to turn a profit from their investment. This pressure can cause them to execute losing trades and they can end up losing their trading capital as a result.

In day trading, intra-day volatility affects not only the entry point, but it can also impact the exit point. When it comes to day trading and short-term strategies, good timing will be the primary determinant of your success or failure in trading.

Long term trading

Long term trading usually involves trading in the forex market by holding a trade position for an extended period of time. This period can range from a couple of weeks to months or years. Position or long-term traders are not active traders. They initiate few trade positions in an entire year. Short-term price fluctuations and the economic news do not have as big an impact on long term trading as they do on short term trading.

Long term traders make use of weekly and monthly price action analysis charts to determine how particular security fluctuates. They make profits and returns from the price changes in the primary trends. Position trading is characterized by trades that are performed with emphasis on both fundamental and technical analysis. These trading indicators give position traders a better evaluation of the forex market, and the ability to make better trade decisions.

Long term traders do not need to look at the market's daily basis because they make long term trades that remain in play for extended periods of time. This means that people with day jobs or other commitments can comfortably engage in long term trading because it does not require constant monitoring.

A trader can choose to have both short-term forex trades and long-term trades as part of a diversified investment strategy. It is important to note that while long term trading offers less action requires little daily monitoring, day trading is a fast-paced, active method of trading that requires a high tolerance for stress and pressure as well as constant vigilance.

Keep a Daily Diary

Keeping a trading diary is primarily used to help you in sticking to your trading plan and strategies. A trading journal is a mechanism that a trader can use in recording their past, current and intended trades. The data captured in the journal provides a means for self-evaluation in terms of the efficacy of the trading strategies used. When you come up with a good trading plan that is well documented, you will be in a position to effectively review your performance, plans, and strategies and determine what works and what doesn't.

The main objective of your trading diary is to allow you to have a detailed account of your trades and their performance in terms of profit or loss and to enable you to gauge the efficacy of your trading plan.

The Two-Part Journal

Your trading journal should:
- Give you a clear record of trades made.
- Have a clear indication of the strategies used to direct a particular trade.

This data will enable you to calculate the reliability of your trading system after observing several trades. When doing your analysis use data from similar strategies to avoid getting inconclusive results that can be caused by having multiple variables in your analysis.

In summary, your diary will serve as a;

1. Planning Tool

A good trade journal will have a record of your actual trade data as well as your intended trades. When you plan ahead for your trades you can put in place mechanisms such as stop loss and take profit limits.

2. Historical Record

Over a period of time of recording your trades in a journal, the journal will provide a historical perspective on your trading patterns. It will summarize all your trades and provide an insight into the state of your trading account.

3. Methodology Verification

A journal is an effective tool that you can use to verify your methodology. By studying your trades over a period of time you can easily determine which strategies deliver favorable results and which ones you need to change because they do not work well.

Chapter 8: Forex Specifics

Proper management of risk exposure is key in any effective forex trading plan. Risk management enables you to determine your entry and exit points from the market. The first step involves being able to select favorable Risk/Reward Ratios for your trades.

Risk-Reward Ratio

A risk-reward ratio measures the difference between entry into the trade and the limit orders you put in place which are the stop-loss and take-profit orders. Setting a risk/reward ratio improves your chances of success in the long run by enabling you to set limit orders that protect your trading capital. For instance, if you are using a risk-reward ratio of 1:2, it means that 50 pips are traded to win 150 pips,

Forex traders determine the expected profits from a particular trade using the RRR. This ratio is will be determined based on the amount a trader will lose in the event that the market goes against his trade and the profit the trader will make if the trade closes in his favor (the reward). The basic principle of the risk-reward ratio in forex trading is to make trades that offer a higher reward than the risk posed.

For effective application of the risk/reward ratio to your trading strategy, the key is to identify a positive ratio for your trade that will effectively limit the amount you stand to lose if the market moves against you. Understanding the RRR can help you avoid falling into a pattern where you lose more on bad trades than you win on good trades. In this situation where the losses are bigger than profits, your RRR is negative.

With 1:2 RRR you can maximize profits on winning trades while at the same time limit potential losses when a trade moves against you. When you are using a 1:2 ratio, it means that you are trading 50 pips to gain 100. This will keep your trading account profitable even if you lose the trade.

You do not need an extremely high win rate or a large RRR to make money as a trader. As long as your risk/reward ratio and your historical win rate match, your trades will provide a positive expectancy.

Table illustrating RRR against Win Rates

Win Rate	Minimum Risk Reward Ratio
25%	3:1
33%	2:1
40%	1.5:1
50%	1:1
60%	0.7:1
75%	0.3:1

Types of Orders

The term order in a foreign exchange context basically refers to how a forex trader enters or exit a trade. Traders use forex orders to manage their trades. Knowing the basic types of orders available will equip you with information and the understanding of when to enter and exit the market appropriately. Common orders in forex trading include:

Market Orders

When an order is made to either buy an asset at the best available price or sell at the prevailing price this is referred to as a market order. In this kind of order entry and exits into trades are done on the basis of the current price available in the market. These kinds of orders are ideal for day traders who usually need to enter and exit trades quickly.

Entry Orders

Orders that allow for an entry position to be placed outside of the prevailing market prices is referred to as an entry order. When the price reaches the determined entry position the entry order is then made and a new position created.

Stop Loss Orders

Orders that are tied to a specific price that is set as the sale price are referred to as stop-loss orders. These kinds of orders designed to minimize possible losses on a trade. Stop-loss orders can be applied in both short term and long-term trades. A stop-loss order is especially useful when one is not able to monitor their trades constantly.

When it comes to stop-loss orders forex traders have two options. Traders can establish stops at a static stop that is fixed at a certain point until the trade is exited or they can use trailing stops that can be changed depending on the direction of the trade.

There are other types of orders in the forex market that are not as popular as the ones listed above. Some of these orders are;

- GTC

A Good Till Cancelled order is used to place an order which will remain active until you give the broker the order to cancel.

- GFD

A Good for the Day is a type of order that closes at the end of the trading day.

- OCO

When a stop-loss order is combined with an entry order, the result is a One Cancels the Other Order. In this situation, the execution of one trade effectively closes the other trade.

Once you decide on the type of order you want to place. You can then proceed to place your order; most brokers will follow the same basic steps for order placement but you can verify with your individual broker for any clarification. The basic steps for placing an order are;

- Open a deal ticket and select the "Order" tab.
- Select either a Buy or Sell trade.

- Specify the price level. This will consequently determine the type of order depending on whether the level is above or below the current market price.
- Place your stops or limits.
- Submit your order.

It is important to familiarize yourself with the trading platform you are working with before undertaking any form of trading activity.

How Many Pips are Enough?

A pip is a unit used to express the difference between two currencies. For instance, I a scenario where an AUD/GBP currency pair moves from 1.1050 to 1.1051, that .0001 then the pip value, in this case, would be 1. Forex brokers will usually work out the pip value for your trades automatically.

Going after a certain number of pips per day may sound like a good plan when trading forex, but it is not an effective trading strategy. Successful traders do not trade with a specific number of pips in mind. This is because markets do not move in a predictable manner, so a trader cannot depend on reaching a targeted number of pips per trade as a trading strategy.

The number of pips per day will vary depending on the strategy adopted as well as the unique goals set by the individual. Certain strategies such as scalping target smaller more frequent profits over multiple trades while other strategies look for large profit-taking opportunities over extended periods of time.

To be successful in forex trading a realistic approach you accept that not all trades will yield positive returns will serve you well. Trying to achieve a daily pip goal is setting yourself up for failure; focusing on a winning strategy should, therefore, be your primary goal when getting into forex trading.

Chapter 9: Plan Your Day

Get Rid of the Fluff

For both novices and seasoned traders in forex, having a stable well thought out forex trading plan is a fundamental principle to adhere to. Success in the forex trade like any other venture requires self-discipline. A trading plan is one of the most effective tools that you can use to stay disciplined in your trading habits and have a logical trading strategy that you can apply to your trades. A well-defined forex trading plan acts as a guide to keep you on a trading path to getting good returns on your investment.

Having a well-defined trading plan means that you can hold yourself accountable to a particular set of standards and goals that you have set. This will improve your trading outcomes by giving you a clear sense of direction to follow. In essence, getting into forex trading without a plan is more or less like gambling and it will cost you in the long run.

A forex trading plan will remind you of the best interests and strategies for your trading account as well as help you in avoiding making decisions based on emotions such as greed, overconfidence or fear. A trading plan will also be a useful tool when you are reviewing your methodologies to establish what works and what does not.

Having a written down account of your trades and the strategies you applied to those trades will provide a historical record of your trading performance. You can routinely review this performance record to see if your strategies are working or whether they should be adjusted to improve trading performance.

An effective forex trading plan should be adhered to during the execution of the trade but can be amended once the market has closed. A trading plan should ideally change with market conditions and be adjusted as your trading skills improve and get better with time and experience in the forex market. For better results write your own trading plan, following a generic plan developed by someone else will not reflect your trading needs or characteristics and might therefore not be an effective way of tracking or mapping out your trading progress.

There are basic features necessary for a comprehensive plan. These are;

Skills

Checking the skills you have that will equip you in trading will help you determine your level of preparedness. The plan should detail what you intend to trade in, preferred trading duration and the overall objectives of your trade. You should also illustrate the strategies you intend to use.

Mental State

Are you mentally ready for trading? Are you feeling confident or nervous? If you feel unprepared after self-assessment, it is better to take the day off to avoid trading when stressed or preoccupied with other things. If you are not in a good mental state you will be more prone to making mistakes.

Having a mantra to repeat before the day begins, physical exercises such as yoga, meditation or deep breathing exercises are a few examples of things you can do to relieve anxiety or stress and put yourself in the right frame of mind before you start trading.

Set Goals or Objectives

Before you start trading you should set out clear goals and realistic objectives. Setting realistic goals is important as it will keep your plan feasible and you will avoid the pitfalls that come with trying to make a fortune overnight like taking uncalculated risks and over-leveraging yourself.

Set Your Risk Level

In much the same way that you will define what your objectives are, it is equally important to establish your risk levels so that you do not deplete your trading capital by lack of risk management strategies. High-risk forex trades may promise great returns but will also increase the probability of losses. This is why risk management is a core factor for success in foreign exchange trading.

Do Your Homework

It is important to keep up with the news and check current affairs trending worldwide that may affect markets. Markets are influenced by economic, political pronouncements and a variety of other factors, therefore, knowing what is happening will aid you as to how the markets are likely to react. Posting a list on the wall or on your computer of expected pronouncements that could impact your trading will serve as a reminder that you can check before you start trading.

Set Exit Rules

If you spend too much time focusing on buying signals and forget to consider or come up with an exit plan you might end up losing profits earned by staying in a trade longer than you should have. While entry points are important knowing when to exit trades should also be given due consideration.

It is important to work with take-profit and stop-loss orders that will direct your entry and exit points to efficiently minimize risks.

Keep Excellent Records

To be good in forex trading you require accurate data. If you win a trade, you should be able to check when and how you won the trade, similarly, when you lose a trade you should know how and when it was lost. These records will help you to avoid repeating trading mistakes that you have made in previous trades as well as in determining which strategies have been the most effective in winning your trades.

Trading records will help in determining the efficacy of a particular strategy.

Review

After each trading day, you should review your trading activities in terms of profit or loss totals as well as understanding the reasons behind them. It is important to note down your observations so that you can use them later.

Cut Out Negative People

By focusing on the logical aspects of trading you will be better equipped to avoid emotional influences such as greed, euphoria, overconfidence or fear.

In forex trading, just like in other spheres of life, you cannot avoid coming into contact with other people. You will meet people in the form of brokers, fellow traders or different people that you interact with on different levels in the course of your trading. While some people are helpful and willing to support and encourage you in your venture, there are also inevitably negative people who will hinder your progress either knowingly or unknowingly.

As we have already established, choosing the right broker will be your most important trade. This is because the wrong broker can seriously damage any chances of your success in forex trading. The forex market like any other field has its fair share of unscrupulous traders and brokers who will take your money and run at the first opportunity.

For any trader in the forex market, it is crucial to ensure that your broker is duly registered by all the relevant authorities. It is also important to check the customer service efficacy of the broker before starting to trade with them by asking questions on email and checking how responsive and helpful they are. This can save you a lot of headaches and unpleasant experiences down the line.

While it is good to compare notes with others and even get a mentor to guide you in your trading journey, it is important to remember that our personal objectives are different. Practices such as adopting someone else's trading plan will reduce your probability of success. A trading plan is most effective when it is made on the basis of your own needs, trading strategies, and objectives.

At the end of the day, forex is a business and should be treated as such. With your money on the line, your primary focus should be on getting good returns on your investments and if these means that you will need to cut off people who will hinder your progress then so be it. Surrounding yourself with like-minded, positive people who share your objectives and goals will be more helpful to you in achieving your trading goals than hanging onto toxic influences and people.

Set Yourself a Goal

A goal is the most important part of any endeavor because it points you in the direction you need to go. A goal is basically your 'why?' You need a 'why 'as to why you're doing this. Your goal should form the main reason and inspiration behind why you're trying to become a successful trader. For instance, your goal for investing in forex trading can be to build your financial independence while working from home, increasing your disposable income or simply expanding or diversifying your investment portfolio.

Your goal is what will effectively direct and guide your trading plan. Trading without a goal in mind is akin to shooting in the dark, once in a while you might hit a target but more often than not when you aim for nothing you are likely to get it. Having a personal goal will keep you focused and ensure that you stay on track even when things are not going in your favor.

When setting your trading goals, it's important to consider the following factors;

Focus on the Process, Not the Results

When you build a strategy based on making a certain amount of money by a specified date and time, you are bound to fail. Setting these kinds of goals will not only cause you emotional stress and undue pressure, but it will also make you more prone to overlooking risks in order to make the specific amount you have set in your mind as an ideal target.

When you focus your efforts on creating a great trading strategy, you will inadvertently ensure success. This is because you will work on improving your strategies which will, in turn, improve your trading skills and eventually result in better returns. When you focus too much on the results you will tend to trade too often and risk too much meaning that you are more likely to suffer losses.

Have a Clear Daily Routine

The routine you follow will have an indirect impact on your trading. Your actions from the morning routine, to the time you go to sleep, will impact your trading performance. Proper mental health and state of mind is a key factor for effective trading in forex or any other venture for that matter. Making sure you are in the right frame of mind and ready to take on the markets will result in better performance. Some of the things you should include in your daily routine are;

- Prepare the night before by getting enough rest so that you are well-rested on the trading day, this will ensure that you stay alert and sharp while trading.
- Energize your body and mind, this will help you to reduce any stress or anxiety and prepare you mentally. You can achieve this through physical exercise, meditation or deep breathing exercises.
- Mentally rehearse what you plan to do, this will make the actual execution easy and flawless since you will have already run through the process in your mind.
- Establish the price action for your markets.
- Plan your trades for the day.

Construct a Process for Analyzing Market Conditions

It is important to have a well-defined process for how you analyze markets that you perform daily and with the daily repetition it will eventually become an automatic habit. You should make a rule to never take a trade unless you have gone through the process fully.

Stay on the Defensive

Protecting your trading capital should be your first priority. This means that you should focus on risk management when trading and this will inadvertently increase your potential of making profits as opposed to losses. To effectively manage your risks and protect the trading capital in your account, you can;

- Set drawdown limits for the month.
- Stay within your level of risk tolerance.

Make Your Goals Progressive

Becoming a great forex trader is all about step by step improvements in your trading as you continually gain experience and skills for better performance. Setting small realistic goals is more effective than setting an unrealistic target for yourself. You can start with small goals that you can then adjust and build on as your trading improves and you get better at making good returns.

Get More Sleep

Sleep deprivation affects your psychological state and mental health. Sleep allows the brain to absorb data that we get throughout the day. Sufficient sleep will go a long way in improving concentration, learning new concepts and staying alert and focused during the day.

Sleep generally impacts on your mental health by;

Improving Your Memory

Our memories are typically formed in three stages. The first stage is the acquisition of information which occurs when you introduce new information to your brain. The second stage is consolidation; this is typically when the memory is strengthened. The final stage in the process is the recall function. This is when we access the information that we stored.

Acquisition and recall stages usually happen when we are awake, while consolidation occurs when we are asleep. When we are sleeping, our brain consolidates and organizes our memories, this helps us to remember what we learned the previous day.

Lowers Your Stress

Research has shown that sleep deprivation makes us more irritable. Irritability makes us prone to over-reacting and getting out of sorts over minor annoyances and interruptions that would in normal circumstances not bother us. A survey from the American Psychological Association found that adults who slept fewer than eight hours a night were more likely to report symptoms of stress than those who slept eight or more hours.

Not getting enough sleep will result in;
- fatigue
- mental fog
- poor decision making

To make sure you are getting enough sleep on a daily basis and thus in a good mental state the following day, you can follow these tips consistently and with time, you will find that the quality of your sleep improves enough for you to get sufficient rest.

- do not linger in bed.
- get up at approximately the same time every day
- get physical exercise
- do not nap during the day, if you have to, do not nap for more than 45 minutes.
- Incorporate physically activity and exercise in your daily routine
- limit your caffeine intake, it is best to avoid caffeine altogether after 4 pm
- Go to bed at the same time every day
- Do not smoke or drinking alcohol right before going to bed
- Before turning in, allow yourself time to wind down
- keep your bedroom quiet, dark, well ventilated and cool

Chapter 10: Tips for Success

With daily transactions in excess of 1.4 trillion US dollars, it is a gold mine for discerning traders. Investors have the potential to make huge profits and losses by engaging in the currency exchange trade. The easy accessibility of this market for both onshore and offshore investors has contributed a great deal to its rising popularity among both seasoned investors and novices in trading.

Forex trading is open 24 hours a day. This makes it one of the most flexible and easily accessible markets. The ease of accessibility of the forex markets is also a great feature for new investors looking for an accessible way to invest and for seasoned traders looking to diversify their investment portfolios.

The foreign exchange market is easy to access regardless of one's country or financial standing. Forex trading gives traders access to average to leverage which means that they have an opportunity to make more with less. Leverage enables traders to borrow money which they can use to boost their trading capital meaning that they are able to generate more returns on their investments.

In the forex trading market, high amounts of leverage are available to the trader which means that they can magnify their returns by using their leverage to increase the potential profits made from a trade.

Although forex trading is a great opportunity for investors to make money and get returns on their trading capital, like any other investment, forex trading does carry the potential for losses. Investment in any venture is a double-edged sword, it carries the potential for returns on capital but there are also the inevitable risks that mean that any trade can result in either profit or loss. It is therefore important to approach forex trading with a realistic mind frame and understand that it takes commitment, time, and continue learning to get maximum returns from your investment.

Safeguarding your money by taking steps to ensure that your investment yields profits should be an investor's primary goal when they start engaging in forex trading. When you venture into investment the aim is primarily to make your money generate more money for you in the form of profits. Yet many investors lose money hand over fist by failing to take the time to understand the markets they are getting into and how best to trade in them. Forex trading should not be treated as a get rich quick scheme but rather as a business that requires well thought out methodologies and strategies to achieve success.

While no investment can be 100% risk-free, taking steps to safeguard your investment and trading wisely will help you to reduce the possibility of making losses and potentially losing your trading capital on bad trades and risky market moves. In any form of trading, your profit opportunities as an investor will always be tied to the comparable risks. Forex trading may be profitable, but it also carries a high level of risk.

Market fluctuations that occur periodically will tend to affect the price of your forex contract and its potential profit or loss. Other factors such as economic releases and policy announcements, political pronouncements and other emerging news might cause market changes and cause trends to change. This means that a potentially good trade can turn bad within seconds and reverse your gains.

Forex trading like any other investment will require commitment and planning to achieve success. Training yourself and equipping yourself with skills in market analysis and risk management will go a long way in ensuring your long-term profitability in forex trade.

Succeeding on Buy and Sell

Just like you should not trade in forex without a solid trading plan, when it comes to buying and selling currency pairs it is crucial to have strategies in place to ensure that you make the most out of your trades. At the core of any trading strategy, is the concept of buying a commodity with the anticipation that it will increase in value, and then it can be sold at a higher cost to make some profit. The difference between your buying price and your selling price will be your profit.

The same principle applies to the selling of commodities. The key strategy in selling is that you will sell the commodity when the value is high, in anticipation that the value will depreciate, and then the commodity can be bought back at a lower price than what it was sold for. Similarly, the difference between your selling price and the buying price will constitute your profit on that particular trade. This concept is the whole principle behind buy and sell.

To develop a winning strategy, before buying or selling, it is important for traders looking to invest to take into account;

- The first step every trader should have in their strategy is to determine the general trend of the market.
- Forex traders should always apply an effective indicator to determine the potential reversal points in the market. This will help in verifying the strength of the trend, i.e. if it is strong, weak, or insignificant.
- The next step will be filtering your signal in the direction of the trend. This means that you should only trade the signals that are generated towards the direction of the trend you have verified.

In addition, there are many different ways of analysis as discussed in previous chapters, that you can use to analyze the foreign exchange market, in anticipation of trading. Using both fundamental and technical analysis techniques either in isolation or in combination will give you a better understanding of the market trends and thus equip you to determine the best buy and sell points to get the maximum returns possible on your trades.

When it comes to fundamental analysis, it will basically involve studying the economic strength of various countries, in order to make well-informed forex predictions. These will require you to be on the lookout for geopolitical and economic events that tend to influence the currency market. On the other hand, technical analysis helps in predicting future trends and price movements in the forex market by examining past market data, particularly in terms of price data.

Patterns in trading will tend to repeat themselves. In turn, these patterns, produced by movements in price, referred to as forex signals, can be used to anticipate market behavior and trends.

Mistakes to Avoid in Forex Trading

Skipping the Trading Plan

Trading without a plan is in effect gambling with your investment and is likely to wipe you out. Plans are essential for success in any business venture and forex trading is no exception to this rule. To become a successful currency trader, you need to have a clear vision, meaning that you should have a good idea of possible market moves, strategies that you will use and the trades you plan to execute.

Overtrading

Overtrading is a common mistake that both novices and seasoned traders make in the forex market. It is usually a result of emotions such as greed where you are trying to reach a specific target and thus end up making more trades than you should. Revenge is also a common factor for over trading where a trader is trying to recover from losses by trading more and more, the net of this is that you end up making even more losses and may eventually wipe out even your trading capital.

To mitigate the effects of over trading, it is important to plan ahead on the number, duration, and frequency of trades that you will make over a certain period of time. This will act as your guide and help you in avoiding the emotional influence that can cause you to trade more than you should.

Over Leveraging

The power of leverage works in two ways, this means it increases your potential losses in much the same way it magnifies your potential profits. Leverage also exposes you to heavier losses because when you over leverage you are in effect playing with more money so in case of a loss you will lose more. Further, leverage is a constant liability to the forex trader because the leverage amount must be paid whether you make profits or loss on your trade. It is also important to remember the leverage attracts interest and in the long term, this cost will accrue.

Determining the correct level of leverage will be instrumental to your trading success. To keep your leverage within acceptable limits and minimize your risk exposure, simply consider the following;

- Use stops to limit exposure.
- Keep trades small.
- Limit capital per trade.

Poor Risk Management

Risk and rewards are natural components in the forex market. Poor risk management leads to losing money in forex trading and it can even mean losing even your trading capital. Making money should be secondary in terms of goals, your primary focus should be holding on to your trading capital because without capital you will essentially be out of business.

Risk management is an essential part of the strategy of any trader who wants to succeed in forex trading. Some basic tips for effective risk management include

- Investing only what you can afford to lose
- Knowing your limits
- Setting a Risk Reward Ratio
- Limiting your risk per trade
- Choosing your leverage wisely
- Keep your risk consistent

Setting the Wrong Goals

Doing things, the right way might net you fewer profits but will be more sustainable in the long term. If you set making money as your only goal, especially at the early stages of your forex trading venture, chasing the money may soon become the very reason for failure. Chasing money will more often than not cause you to break the rules of your trading plan in an attempt to make more money faster.

Breaking these rules may once in a while you net you some profits but in the long run, it almost always leads to an empty trading account balance. Instead of focusing only on how much money you need to make within a certain period, focus instead on your strategies and processes. By improving your trading skills and strategies consistently you will inadvertently end up making money using good trading practices. Like most endeavors, in forex trading, the process is ultimately more important than the results in the long term.

Ignoring the Psychological Aspect of Trading

Psychology plays a big role in terms of avoiding making mistakes in trading forex. Emotions are a normal and ever-present factor in the human experience and pretending that negative or positive emotions will not influence your trading decisions and patterns are simply self-delusion. Understanding market psychology and yourself is a good starting point in recognizing and overcoming this mistake.

We have already looked at how overconfidence, fear, anxiety, and greed can impact your trading. It is therefore important to develop and adhere to a trading plan so that you avoid making emotional decisions when trading the market.

Giving up

Most traders who approach the forex market as a means of making a quick fortune eventually give up when they realize that success will not come overnight. It may be cliché, but good things really do come to those who wait. Provided that you risk only what you can afford to lose, patience, persistence, and determination to succeed will eventually pay off and make your forex trading investment worthwhile.

It is unrealistic to expect that you will become a trading expert overnight so if you quit or give up at the first challenge you face you will be likely to be throwing away a potentially lucrative investment opportunity. It is prudent to await the growth of your skills and methodologies; this will come with the more experience and exposure that you will gain with time in the forex market.

Conclusion

Thank you for making it through to the end of *Forex Trading for Beginners*, let's hope it was informative and able to provide you with all of the tools and information you need to start your journey in the foreign exchange market trade.

Investment requires discipline, patience, and commitment in order to achieve the maximum returns from your capital. By implementing the skills and strategies you have learned in this book you can develop a sound trading plan that will chart your way to success in forex trading.

Taking advantage of this extensive global market that is foreign exchange will increase your money-making opportunities and open you up to learning new ways of multiplying your money. By using your disposable income to generate more money you will be in effect ensuring your financial future and creating a path to a wealthy and financially stable future.

Taking charge of your life when it comes to finances means that you will be willing to take calculated risks in an effort to make your money work for you. Investment is a double-edged sword that creates the opportunity for making either loss or profit on your capital. Provided you follow the guidelines provided in this book on risk management, your forex trading investment is bound to be a success in the long term.

By reading this book you have already taken the first step towards improving your knowledge in forex trading and equipped yourself with the tools you will need to get started. The next step is to start incorporating the strategies and critical tips recommended in this book and take your first move into forex trading. Let's hope that you will start realizing the benefits of Forex trading soon.

Finally, if you found this book useful, a review on Amazon is always appreciated.

The End

www.ingramcontent.com/pod-product-compliance
Lightning Source LLC
Chambersburg PA
CBHW072024230526
45466CB00019B/256